THROUGH

At Monum

By: Lucille Lavelett

I extend my sincere thanks and appreciation to Marian M. McDonough of Palmer Lake for letting me use the files of the late Lloyd McFarling, who had started a historical book of Monument, Colorado.

I also wish to thank Florence Brandt Armstrong, the granddaughter of Henry Limbach; Clifton Lierd, the son of Will Lierd; Florence Rupp Glendening, daughter of Dr. Rupp; Dr. Frances McConnell Mills, daughter of Dr. McConnell; Wilber Fulker; Alice Schubarth Wright; Lela Dolan Hagedorn, granddaughter of Henry Guire; Elsie Pettigrew Shanks; Ramona Brown Wissler; Melvin Olson; Mr. and Mrs. Fred Lewis, who gave me pictures and valuable information; to Shirley Mumm, town clerk, who let me use Monument's first two minute books; and to Marion Fletcher for typing copy for printing.

My thanks and appreciation to Jim Allis who redeveloped many of the pictures for me.

Published By:
Palmer Lake Historical Society (PLHS)
P.O. Box 662, Palmer Lake, CO. 80133

Editing, layout, & photo scans by Rogers M. Davis.
Indexing and research by Herbert "Hobie" Edwards.
OCR scanning of text by Victor Vaile.

Suggested Cataloging Data

Lavelett, Lucille

Through the Years at Monument, Colorado: The story of
Monument Colorado / by Lucille Lavelett – 5th edition

Includes index.

ISBN 0-9755989-0-2 (pbk.)

168 pages, Illustrated, Revised and Expanded

1. Frontier and pioneer life – Colorado.

2. Monument, Colorado -History. I Title.

Cover Photos:

Front Cover:

Monument Rock, Colorado, is the local rock formation the town of
Monument derived its name from – ca 1885. Photo courtesy of Ralph
& Norma Lavelett.

Back Cover:

George Betz, center-front passenger seat, and his chain drive delivery
truck. A close look at the wheels reveals that the tires are hard-rubber.
Still, this truck with its springs was a better ride than the horse-drawn
delivery wagon in use just a year or two before this photo was taken –
ca 1913 -14 Mr. Betz was owner of a Monument meat market.

Photos: from the Lucretia Vaile Museum, Palmer Lake CO. Other Photos
are courtesy of the Colorado Springs Pioneers Museum, the Castle Rock
Museum, Ralph & Norma Lavelett, M. Korbitz, Ted Colley, Roger & Susan
Davis, Bill Simpson, Violetta Fauver, and the Tri-Lakes Fire Department.

*I dedicate these pages to all my friends near and far
who have helped me write this book.*

Lucille Lavelett

Mrs. Anna Judd wrote this poem in 1940. Anna Judd lived in this community for many years. She was a true Christian, a loyal friend to everyone, and a helpful person to the community. When the Homemakers made their scrap-book she wrote the poem and dedicated it to the pioneers of Monument who blazed the trail, bore the hardships and endured the suffering that we might have better homes, more of the comforts and pleasures of life.

May we never forget them for all we have now is memories.

"OUR PIONEERS"

They rode ahead and blazed the trail
In covered wagon trains
They saw the sunset of the West
Across the rolling plains.
They fashioned rude homes of the sod
And tilled the virgin soil
Those pioneers were staunch and strong
In hope and faith secure
They conquered all, endured the pain,
And builded homes to God.

By: Anna Judd.

Contents

Editors Note

In preparing this book for reprinting, the goal was not to rewrite Mrs. Lavelett's book as much as it was to reorganize the book making it friendly to the reader. To that end, I have chosen a larger font and placed more white-space between the lines. All photographs and documents were rescanned and digitally enhanced to bring out the best image possible. Many new photographs were added that were not available to Mrs. Lavelett. When text was changed that change was only intended to place in context, update, or clarify the sentiments or facts expressed. If a topic/chapter was added I felt that this addition was necessary to establish correct context or to correct an omission from the original book.

Mr. "Hobie" Edwards made an index for the book consisting of well over five-hundred-fifty entries. That index will prove very helpful to those wishing to find reference to a particular person. A table of contents has been added to aid in navigating to a particular topic. Most of the 130 + photographs and illustrations have been dispersed throughout the book and placed with the topic that the photographs relate to. There is still a Gallery of Photographs containing many fine photos that pertain to the history of Monument which were not included with the text for one reason or another.

I believe that this volume remains true to the original book while greatly enhancing the reader's historical experience. Finally, the book is primarily concerned with the first hundred years of Monument history as was Mrs. Lavelett's intent.

My thanks to The Monument Homemakers Club, Herbert "Hobie" Edwards, Victor Vaile, Susan Davis, and all that had a hand in preparing this volume for reprinting.

Rogers M. Davis
Director, Vaile Museum

{ vii }

Through The Years
At Monument, Colorado

The Story of Monument, Colorado
Covering the First 100 Years.

Lucille Lavelett

DISCOVERY & MAPPING

M onument Creek rises in the Rampart Range of the Rocky Mountains about sixty miles southwest of Denver. It emerges from the mountains just south of the Platte-Arkansas Divide at the Town of Palmer Lake and flows in a southeastern and southern direction until it empties into Fountain Creek within the City of Colorado Springs. From Palmer Lake to Colorado Springs the creek meanders along the eastern edge of a valley from one to six miles wide, bordered on the west by the Rampart Range and on the east by a rolling plateau somewhat higher than the valley level, partly covered by a pine forest known in the early days as the Pineries but more recently called the Black Forest.

This valley was explored by the Long Expedition of 1820, the Dodge Expedition of 1835, and the Fremont Expedition of 1843. Long's party discovered the white and lavender Columbine, flower in the area, which would later become the Colorado state flower in 1899. Dodge mapped the stream as *Fontaine Que Bouillait,* and Fremont called it the eastern fork of the *Fontaine-qui-Bouit,* but on the Preuss map, published with Fremont's report, it was designated as Monument Creek. The name was probably derived from the monument-like rocks found at several places in the valley.

In the early 1860's ranchers began to acquire land in the valley of Monument Creek. Some of this land was taken up under the Homestead Act of 1862, but most of it was purchased from the federal government under various laws at $1.25 per acre. Most of the purchasers were land speculators who sold their holdings to bona fide settlers, later, at higher prices.

-- Lloyd McFarling

The William Bangs Young campsite somewhere on the Great Plains while traveling to CO. - 1871. Settled in the Husted area.

Photo courtesy of Roger & Susan Davis. Artist: W. B. Young

THE EARLY SETTLERS

*M*onument, Colorado is located approximately twenty miles north of Colorado Springs, and approximately fifty miles south of Denver.

Some of the first people to settle in and around Monument came from Iowa. There were the Guires; John, Henry, Jacob, Joe, and Dave. David McShane, the Weltys, Roberts, Walkers, Andrew Demasters, and C. E. Chaloner.

My grandfather Olfs came from Germany in 1860.
Henry Limbach came from Germany in 1866.
The Richard Gwillims came from Neath, South Wales to Colorado in 1869.

The Gwillim brothers had a general merchandise store in Monument in 1878 and founded the community called Gwillimville, which was five miles east of Monument.

The wagon trains of pioneers brought many of their possessions with them including candle molds, coffee mill, and one wagon load of flour which Henry Guire sold for $18.00 per hundred to pay expenses across the plains. They also had in their train covered wagons drawn by oxen, two milk cows tied behind. They put the milk in containers in the wagon and the jolting of the wagon churned the milk into butter.

The first settlers brought willow cuttings with them. They kept the cuttings in barrels of water to keep them alive and when settled on their homesteads planted them. They have grown to some of the largest, finest trees in this area. At some of the homes these trees were still growing in 1974. Some may still be seen at the former homes of Henry Guire, and John Dolan, also the Joe Guire home, the David McShane home, and the Dave Guire home.

All of the families helped each other build their homes. The Guire and McShane homes were made of stone with two-foot thick walls, which were plastered inside, and outside. The doors were narrow, and the windows were recessed deep with portholes in case of Indian attacks. The McShane house was still a livable home until it was replaced in the late 1990s. It was the oldest house in this area. The first settlers had to be alert at all times for Indians. A circular stone fort was built on the McShane ranch in 1865-68. It was twelve feet in diameter with stone walls two feet thick and a roof of logs. Earth covered the logs to prevent Indians from setting the roof on fire. There were five portholes of which four of them had sliding blocks of stone to close them. The fifth porthole was really a window. It gave the only light and faced the McShane house. From this porthole the families could see if any Indians were creeping up on the house. An underground passage led from the house to the fort.

Every day a man rode out to a high hill just north and west of the fort to be on the lookout for Indians. This hill is still called the "Look-Out". When the lookout man saw Indians in the distance he would inform the people, then all would hurry to the McShane fort.

Isabella Trigg and her brother Jack Martin were among the early pioneers to live here. Isabella Trigg was a large woman weighing about two hundred and fifty pounds. From all information I have obtained about her, she was a very helpful and kind woman to all the families living here. She saved the life of one of Jacob Guire's children from an Indian one day.

Several families had been at the fort for several days for protection from the Indians. It had been quiet and peaceful for a day, so the boy was let out to play. Isabella Trigg looked out and saw an Indian riding over the hill. She dashed out, grabbed the boy, pushed him into the fort, and slammed the port hole shut just as the Indian threw his tomahawk, with the tomahawk embedding in the heavy timber. Isabella Trigg is buried in the Monument cemetery. For many years the only marker on her grave was a white marble bible. While my grandmother Olfs and Mrs. Alice Guire Dolan lived they always put flowers on her grave in memory of the brave, helpful person she was to all the pioneers.

One day the Indians took three hundred horses from several of the families.

The Walker family, who lived north of Monument fled in haste to the fort, their lives were saved but when the Walkers returned to their home it had been burned.

Many times Indians would camp in the Guire meadow (in 1974 the meadowland of the Collier home.) Bands of the Utes would stop at the Guire home for biscuits and syrup. The shepherd dog and one of the horses would always warn Mrs. Guire when the Indians were near. One day she was warned by the dog and horse and she saw some young braves coming toward the house. She didn't like their looks so she hid the children. One of the braves bolted into the kitchen and demanded that she give him some matches. She told the brave she had none. "Heap big lie" the Indian yelled pointing to a box in the windowsill. He started to fit an arrow to his bow, and Mrs. Guire snatched up a flat iron from the stove and started to hurl it at him. The Indian ducked and backed out of the door yelling "Heap big brave squaw" and joined the rest of the Indians and rode away.

In the early 1860's the Indians would hide in the pine timbers east of Monument and wait for an opportunity to make raids on the Monument farms.

One day Mr. McShane had gone to Colorado Springs for their winter supplies of groceries and Mrs. McShane and a part Indian woman by the name of Mrs. Fricks were at home and saw that a group of Indians had come to the farm and were hiding behind a hay stack. They hid the children under the bed. Each got a gun and stood in the doorway pointing the guns at the Indians. Once in a while the Indians came out from the haystack and made the motions of scalping them.

Neither of the women knew much about a gun and one of them accidentally fired their gun. This probably saved their lives. The Indians jumped on their horses and galloped over the hill. The Indians must have thought there were men at home, but as they left they took all the horses with them.

At the Henry Guire home, which was just one mile east of Monument, the first community Christmas tree in the Monument settlement was decorated and the children given their only gifts of cookies, candy, and apples and told the beautiful story of the birth of Christ.

On February 18, 1950 the pioneer courage eulogized as a fort marker was dedicated. The regents of the Zebulon Pike and Kinnikinnik chapter of the American Revolution presented the marker for the historical site to Colorado. The historical marker is on Highway 105 between Monument and Palmer Lake. The fort is 610 feet south of the marker. The plaque on the granite boulder reads, "Old stone fort built at the pioneer home of David McShane" constructed as a defense against Arapahoe and Cheyenne raiders. It was used in 1865 to 1868 as a refuge by the following pioneer families: The Guires, Browns, Jacksons, Shielders, Chandlers, McShanes, Oldhams, Teachouts, Davidsons, Walkers, Demasters, Roberts, Watkins, Faulkners, Simpsons, and Weltys. As related, by Dixie McShane-Woodworth, the fort once had forty people taking refuge inside those cramped quarters at one time.

McShane Fort – ca 1880 minus it's roof.
The window/firing port faced south toward the McShane home.
(See the David McShane addendum on page 146.)

MONUMENT - IN THE BEGINNING

*H*enry Limbach's name appears in an entry book for township 11-67. This book can be found in the Colorado Land Office of the Dept. of the Interior at Denver. Limbach made a first payment on Oct. 1, 1870 on 160 acres of land located partly in Section 5 extended north into Section 10 and 11. The tract was patented to Maria Linder, who was Henry's mother-in-law.

Monument was first called Henry's Station after Henry Limbach. When the Rio Grande railroad was built through here in 1871, the railroad and Henry Limbach changed the name to Monument after the beautiful rock formation to the west. Monument Rock stands high and can be plainly seen from the town.

Mt. Herman, the large mountain west of Monument over-shadowing Monument Lake, was named after one of the pioneers, Herman Schwanbeck, who came from Germany and homesteaded just east of town. (Where the Village Inn Pancake House now stands).

The first Rio Grande train came through Monument January 1, 1872 and A. Trew Blachly was the first station agent. He was chosen to be the agent by General William Jackson Palmer, because Trew was an honest temperance man, and very active in the betterment of the living habits of the town.

The first records of the town can be found in Book 39, Page 53, in the El Paso County Court House, also Book K, Page 32. It records to Charles Adams, July 10, 1872, Territory of Colorado, United States of America.

Charles Adams was born Karl Adams Schwanbeck in Germany in 1845. He came to the United States as a young man and served in the Union Army during the Civil War and afterwards was a cavalryman on the Western Plains. He was appointed Brigadier General of the Colorado Militia in 1870.

Later he was an Indian agent, a special agent in the post-office department and Minister to Bolivia. After the Ute outbreak in 1879 he distinguished himself by entering the territory of the Indians and persuading them to release their white captives.

He was married to an English girl who did not like the German name of Schwanbeck, so had it changed to Charles Adams.

(caption) Mrs. Lucy Carson, a daughter of David McShane who was born in the stone house a few feet from the old stone fort; and Eugene Gammon, who at one time lived at Ramah, Colorado. Mr. Gammon was the first Caucasian child born in the Northeastern El Paso County. They were examining an old army cartridge belt. The belt was worn by Mr. Gammon's father who served at Denver and at Bijou Basin, north of Peyton. The Troops at that time were detailed to keep control of the Indians.

Left to right: Lt. Governor W. E. Higby; Dorothy Buren, D.A.R. Historian; Dr. LeRoy R. Haven, State Historian; Mrs. Roy Davis, regent of Zebulon Pike chapter of D.A.R.; and Mrs. John Crouch, Vice-regent of Kinnikinnik Chapter

Joe Pettigrew, George Stamm at Pat Murphy's cabin - built 1870.

Charles Adams (Schwanbeck) never lived here but owned much land in Monument. He lived in Manitou, Colorado. He died in Denver in 1895 during a fire and explosion at the Gurney Hotel.

January 5, 1874, Charles Adams and Henry Limbach filed with the clerk and recorder plat statements of the town consisting of about sixty acres in the north half of the South-East quarter. 108 lots were platted. Limbach owned 36 and Charles Adams 72. Addition No.1 was platted in 1874 by Henry Limbach, Charles Adams, Charles Baker, and A. F. Woodward. This addition enlarged the town on the north, east, and south adding 136 more lots. Addition No.2 was platted in 1878 by Charles Adams and Henry Limbach and recorded in 1879. It consisted of two blocks between Front Street and the Rio Grande right-of-way, west of the original town. There were two more additions in 1887 and 1888 and one in 1889. Since 1950 several additions to the north and south, and west have been added.

Henry Limbach was born in Germany, Nov. 17, 1842. He arrived from Germany in 1863. He served in Company C of the Forty-first New York Volunteer Infantry during the Civil War. He came West in 1866 as a member of the Eighth Cavalry in which he enlisted to take part in the Indian War. He had the rank of captain. Later he became a true friend to the Indians. He and Chief Ignacio were very close friends. Mr. Limbach took an active interest in politics in El Paso County. He was a good businessman and he and his mother-in-law, Maria Linder owned much of the land in and around Monument. Maria Linder is buried in the Monument Cemetery. Henry Limbach lived in Monument continuously until 1909 when he moved to Denver. He died June 1. 1918.

Caroline Linder Limbach was born in Hilburghausen, Saxony, Germany on May 22, 1842. She came to America with her mother, Mrs. Linder in May 1872. They stopped temporarily in St. Louis, Missouri. There by pre-arrangement, she was met, and married to, Henry Limbach, who had been a companion and schoolmate of her childhood and early youth in Germany. Immediately after marriage she came with her husband; her mother accompanying them, to his ranch which had just been made a station called Henry Station on the D&RG railroad then just built. The country around was still unsettled, only a few ranches near and the bride still unable to speak a word of English. She commenced her new life in a new, strange, and barren-looking country. Caroline Limbach was the first white female resident in Monument. Her eldest son, Ed Limbach, was the first child born in the town. When he was born, it was the first white baby the Indians had ever seen and they would come in droves to look in the windows to see him. The Indians were always friendly but that didn't keep fear out of the mother's heart.

Mrs. Limbach was prominent in church and charitable work, a member of the Presbyterian Church, and active supporter of church and Sunday school. She was active in school matters and at the election in 1893 was elected to the Board of Directors as secretary. She was the proprietor of a large dry goods, millinery, and dressmaking store, which she conducted for twelve years. This building was on the west corner of Front Street and north of Second Street.

Mr. and Mrs. Limbach were the parents of six children; two daughters and four sons. Caroline Limbach passed away May 3, 1894 at age 51 years, 11 months and 11 days. She is buried in the Monument Cemetery.

Caroline Limbach

Henry Limbach

Mrs. Limbach's Dry Goods & Millinery Store, NW corner of
Second & Front St. – ca 1880.

Looking east on Second St. from Front St. – ca 1900.
The stone Walker Bldg. is on the left. Mon. Hotel on the right.

The South end of Front Street also known as Five-Points to the pioneers. The Monument Hotel is the larger building left of center.

MONUMENT INCORPORATED

*I*n the matter of incorporation of the town of Monument, this can be found and verified in Book 39, Page 53 in the El Paso County Court House. It was platted in 1874. On May 5, 1879 the County Court appointed commissioners to proceed according to the law Notice of Election published four times consecutively in newspapers in the limits of the proposed incorporated town. The election was held June 2, 1879. There being seventeen votes for and three votes against. Notice of incorporation was published two weeks in each local newspaper commencing June 2, 1879, ending June 14, 1879. This was certified May 10, 1881 by J. E. McIntyre, clerk of County Court.

The first town minutes books are hard-back paper and written -in longhand. The first meeting was held July 3, 1879 in the Gwillim hall which was on the corner of Third and Front Streets.

Henry Limbach was the first Mayor and A. F. Woodward the first recorder. The first trustees were Richard Gwillim, P. E. Bainter, F. B. Hanscomb and Charles Tiner. At the first meeting W. E. Holbrook was unanimously elected Town Marshall.

The second meeting was held July 10, at the Monument Hotel. P. E. Bainter was elected Town Treasurer, and instructed to give bonds of one thousand dollars. These meetings were during the day and were mainly for drawing up their ordinances. At the third meeting J. D. Woodruff was unanimously elected Town Magistrate. At the fifth meeting, which was July 14, 1879 the first liquor, license applications of Robert Miller and C. S. Tiner were read and approved, and granted to them.

The Board decided not to hold regular meetings, but at the call of the Mayor when needed. Liquor licenses were $250.00 a year. At the Nov. 19, 1879 meeting held in P. E. Bainter's store, A. T. Blachly who was editor of the Monument Mentor newspaper turned in a bill for $75.00 for advertising the town ordinances. According to the minutes, the Board watched the town's money very closely for they only allowed $65.00 for

Blachly's bill. The town Marshall turned in a bill for his services for $19.80 and after considerable discussion the bill was reduced to $14.20 and allowed.

W. B. Walker, or "Rod" as he was called, was the town's second Mayor and John W. Guire, recorder or clerk.

W. B. Walker built a large stone store on the corner of Front and Second Streets in 1880. This building had a large hall up stairs where meetings and dances were held, and had a large potato storage cellar. W. B. Walker owned the entire block between Washington and Front Streets.

R. C. Elliott's name appears in the town's minutes of Aug. 4, 1880 when he was appointed Trustee in the place of George Armstrong. R. C. Elliott was a prominent man in Monument and for many years owned and operated a store on Front Street. He and his partner, J. W. Mudge, opened his store in 1879. He was Town Clerk from May 1887 to April 1896.

Will Lierd came to Monument in 1870 as a tubercular. In 1872 he bought a ranch of 280 acres north and east of Monument on the Douglas County line. He farmed for ten years, then came to Monument and built a store. The store was on 243 Washington Street where the Monument Volunteer Fire Department was in 1974 and the High Country Store is in 2004. The sign on the store read "Dry Goods, shoes, groceries, caskets and coffins. Established in 1882". Men's socks sold for three pairs for 25 cents, a good pair of shoes, $2.50. Hard candy had its own special showcase; plug tobacco was also a big seller with a special cutter on the counter to cut off a plug. On each pound strip of tobacco were five tin horseshoes or stars, which were good for premiums. If a customer didn't want the horseshoes Mr. Lierd would ask for them. Will Lierd's son, Clifton, told me the Lierd's had a dining set acquired by sending in 70,000 horseshoes.

"W. B. Walkers" Store, corner Front & Second St. - ca 1885.
Later became the Monument State Bank from 1917 - 1924.

R. C. Elliott's Mercantile on Front St. - ca 1886.

Photo courtesy of M. Korbitz

Fanny Mudge-Elliott   R. C. Elliott

Elliott photos courtesy of M. Korbitz.

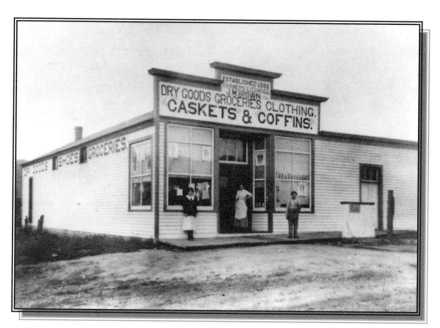

Will Lierd's Store later owned by J. M. Brown – ca 1889.
The store was located at 243 Washington Street.

WATER

*T*he citizens of Monument were very concerned about water for their community. For several years each family had a dug well in their back yard with hand drawn buckets to bring the water to the tap. In the early 1880's the citizens had civic progress and created a bonded debt. It was small at first but it grew and was cared far, extended and kept alive far twenty years, until the interest payments exceeded the principal more than 50%.

Old records show a stock company was promoting a ditch in 1874 to bring water into Monument for irrigation. News reports were that the ditch was partly dug in 1875. Apparently it was abandoned within a few years.

On Sept. 19, 1881 the Town Council decided to call a special election as soon as practicable for the purpose of bringing water into town and issuing bonds far that purpose. The election was held an Oct. 25th. The vote was not recorded but it evidently was favorable for on Nov. 21 the Council passed a resolution authorizing the issuance of $2,500.00 worth of bonds. The bonds were dated Jan. 2, 1882. On March 1, 1882 a contract was awarded to George Newbrough for the construction of the ditch far $1,650.00 and soon other contracts were made for installing a flume in the upper end of the ditch, and for building bridges. On March 27, 1884 Charles D. Ford and Henry Limbach were appointed to make a plan and have ditch recorded. On May 22, 1885 a plat and statement of the priority of the Monument ditch was recorded in Book 60, pages 35 and 36. The ditch ran in an Easterly direction from a point an Monument Creek about two miles northwest-west of Monument and within the present limits of Palmer Lake, to a reservoir in the southwest quarter of Section 11, then turned southwest to another reservoir in the northwest-west quarter of Section 14.

In the Town minutes, the ditch bonds of 1882 carried an interest rate of 8%, which amounted to $200.00 a year. This was regularly paid. Some years later the Council began talking of setting up a sinking fund for the purpose of paying off the principal. On Oct. 7, 1895 the Council adopted an ordinance refunding the entire issue of $2,500.00 at 6% interest. The debt was finally paid off in 1901.

On April 9, 1888 the Council adopted an ordinance granting permission to A. F. Woodward to lay pipes along the streets and alleys, and other public places in the town and sell water there from. It was reported in the Colorado Springs weekly gazette on April 28, 1888 that A. F. Woodward recently laid 1,000 feet of pipe in the Woodward addition to the Town of Monument. The houses in the addition are connected with pipe that was supplied with water from a well, which was brought to the surface by a large windmill. The well was 60 feet deep and 8 feet wide. The tank from which water was drawn had a capacity of 75 barrels. Water for irrigation was used from the Monument ditch.

On June 11, 1911 a special election was held for voting bonds for $2,500.00 to improve the water system. This bond passed. Moss Chandler was Mayor. Trustees were R. E. Reasoner, Dan Davison, N. T. Ingle, Ben Millwright, Guy Schubarth, and Birch Brawner. Andrew Curry was Town Clerk, and Dr. Rupp was Treasurer.

In 1923 the water supply became inadequate and a 420-foot well was drilled in the north end of town near Fifth Street and a new pump house was built. A gas engine was used to bring water to the surface. This time the town was bonded for $7,000.00. This new well had exceptionally pure water and was capable of producing 60 gallons per minute. The town board members in 1923 were W. E. Higby, Mayor; Dr. W. H. Rupp, Treasurer; Andrew Curry, Clerk and Recorder. Trustees were A. E. Fox, W. F. Fulker, A. W. Thompson, Ben Millwright, J. M. Umberger, and Olaf Johnson.

In March 1936 Monument retired its bonded debt of $7,500.00 borrowed in 1923.

At a special meeting called by Mayor W. E. Higby it was voted to retire the balance of the town's original debt. This was the first time the town was out of debt. The town board members at this time were W. E. Higby, Mayor, and Trustees were R. J. Hasstedt, Harry Barnhardt, W. I. Newbrough, Clarence N. Lavelett, B. E. Jack, and F. W. Simpson.

In 1935 water rates were 75 cents a month for meter charge plus 15 cents per thousand gallons.

In 1955 a new well was dug on the northeast-east corner of Monument. W. E. Higby donated this ground. The Town minutes of April 14, 1955 state "in consideration of Higby deeding ground for well site and right-or-way easement, the town relinquishes all further claim of reservoir and ditch claim within his land. This was passed by the Town Council.

This well is 985 feet deep. In 1973 another well was drilled just east of the Santa Fe tracks at the beginning of Second Street. This well is 1848 feet deep. Water rates in 1974 are $6.50 for four thousand gallons, and 50 cents a thousand for each additional one thousand gallons.

MONUMENT RESERVOIR

*I*n 1889 the citizens of Monument were working on a project to build a dam or lake on Monument Creek west of Town. David McShane owned the land where the lake was built. David McShane was given the contract to build the dam. Some of the money to build the dam was raised by public subscription. In 1891 the Colorado Assembly appropriated $30,000.00 or as much of that amount as might be necessary for construction of the dam to store water for the purpose of irrigation, and good of the people for recreation, fishing, and swimming.

When W. E. Higby was Lieutenant Governor of Colorado he was influential in getting the State to deed the lake to the Town. Mr. Higby thought it would be of more benefit if it belonged to the Town. The town owns access to the lake and fifty-feet of land from the high-water mark all the way around the lake.

The reservoir dam needed extensive repairs with the work being completed in 2002. Water rights issues are a concern in that the water needed to fill the reservoir 'belongs' to downstream users, should they place a 'call' on the water to be stored there. The town is struggling for a method to allow the filling of the reservoir. Drought conditions may persist through 2004.

Monument Reservoir Spillway – ca 1902.
Photo courtesy of Ralph & Norma Lavelett.

STREET LIGHTS

M onument's first streetlights were coal oil lanterns on posts. In the minutes of Feb.1, 1892 R. C. Elliott and John Dickinson were appointed as a committee to purchase streetlights. Three lights were purchased. One was put on the corner of Front and Second, one on Second and Washington, and one on Third and Jefferson Streets. The Town paid $19.35 for these lights. In the minutes of May 1,1892 the Town agreed to furnish oil for all private street lights put up by the owner of property, and the Marshall attend and light them the same as the public lights. In 1895 the Marshall was paid $8.00 a month to light the lights every night, blow them out every morning, and keep them in good operating condition. The Town furnished the oil, globes, and wicks.

In 1931 a franchise was granted to Dwight Chapin to furnish electric lights, heat, and power to the Town of Monument. This was the first time Monument had electricity.

The franchise was transferred from Dwight Chapin Jr., to Mountain Utilities Corporation on July 3, 1933.

DRY GOODS & COFFINS

T he P. E. Bainter store was on Front Street, south of the hotel in the area pioneers called Five Points.

J. E. Smith was the first to own the store, which later was the Higby Mercantile, now the Chapala Bldg. Mr. Smith had coffins for sale at his store. The coffins were kept upstairs in a storage attic, which had a drop door on which the coffins could be pushed out. George Sharrock, uncle to Dixie McShane Woodworth, rented this building and operated a store in the 1890's.

J. F. Roth had a store in this building just prior to the Higby's.

This Monument Business Directory gives a good picture of the town that it was; a busy, prosperous, self-supporting town:

MONUMENT BUSINESS DIRECTORY

1875

Colorado Business Directory Annual, Reg. 1876, Monument, El Paso County.

D&RG Railway
Daily Mail
Hotel Monument House ....Mrs. F. R. Ford, proprietor
General Mdse.....................................W. B. Walker
Physician...F. C. Blachly
A Methodist Church is in course of erection.
A Town and Masonic Hall about to be built.

Signed A. Poole, Secy. of Colony.

MONUMENT, COLORADO BUSINESS DIRECTORY

1876
J. A. Blake, Publisher

D&RG Railway.....................................A. T. Blachly, Agent
Population 100
Western Union Telegraph
Daily Mail
Good wagon road to Bergess Park & Fairplay
Distance to Colorado Springs 20 miles
Methodist Church ....Rev. J. L. Dyer
Baptist Church
Postmaster ....Henry Limbach
R. Road & telegraph agent ....A. T. Blachly
Blacksmith...J. J. Leach
Hotel Monument House ....Dr. Robertson

General Mdse. three stores operated by:

> A. T. Blachly
> Henry Limbach
> W. B. Walker

1877 same as in 1876

1878

Postmaster..................................... Henry Limbach
Justice of the Peace .... J. W. Carnahan
Express and R. R. Agent..................... A. T. Blachly
Baptist Church.................................. Rev. T. Mitcheli, Pastor
Methodist Church.............................. T. P. Cook
Prep. Church .... H. B. Gage
Blacksmith .... Chandler & Badger
Boots and Shoes .... Henry Teachout
Carriage Shop .... J. H. Fordle
Cheese Factory.................................. Gwillim Brothers
Contractor & Builder......................... O. B. Dunlap
Drugs.. A. T. Blachly
General mdse.................................... Gwillim Brothers
Henry Limbach W. B. Walker
 Groceries.. P. A. Duncan
Hotel Monument House.................... F. R. Ford
Physician .... Henry Cook
Saw Mill .... N. E. Cornwall

1879
(The year Monument was incorporated)

Baptist Church.................................. Rev. G. B. Armstrong
Drugs.. A. T. Blachly
Physician .... F. C. Blachly
Bottle Beer....................................... John Caylor
Justice of Peace .... J. W. Carnahan
Blacksmith .... M. Chandler & McCall
Physician .... Henry Cook
Methodist Church.............................. T. P. Cook

President of School Board .... Oscar Dunlap
Builder .... O. B. Dunlap
Carriage Shop .... Mr. Farkle
Builder .... W. B. Dyker
Hotel .... Mr. Ford
Cheese Factory .... G. R. Gwillim & Bros.
General Mdse .... Gwillim Bros.
Postmaster .... Henry Limbach
Lumber .... Henry Limbach
General Mdse .... Henry Limbach
Saloon .... Robert Miller
Builder .... M. C. Porter
Boots and Shoes .... Gus Ross
Monument Mentor .... Newspaper
Boots and Shoes .... Henry Teachout
Saloon .... J. F. Tiner & Co.
General Mdse .... J. F. Tiner
Gen. Mdse. & Hides & Pelts .... W. B. Walker
Builder .... George Zimmerman
Presp. Church .... Chas. A. Taylor

1880
Same introduction except Population 200

Town Officers
Mayor .... Henry Limbach
Recorder .... A. F. Woodward
Town Trustees .... P. E. Bainter
                                                              F. B. Hanscomb
                                                              C. S. Tiner
                                                              R. J. Gwillim
Methodist Church .... Rev. G. B. Armstrong
  (Also public school teacher) Drugs ... A. Trew Blachly
Groceries .... P. E. Bainter
Justice of the Peace .... J. W. Carnahan
Blacksmith .... Moses Chandler

Builder .... O. B. Dunlap
Physician .... H. Eddy
General Mdse .... Elliott & Mudge
Cheese Factory.................................... Elliott & Mudge
Boots and Shoes .... P. K. Elliridge
Hotel .... Mrs. F. R. Ford
Baptist Church .... Rev. G. A. Hutinson
Secy. of School Board .... Wm. Lierd
Postmaster and Notary Public .... Henry Limbach
Millinery.. Mrs. C. H. Limbach
Saloon .... Robert Miller
Monument Hotel.................................. Hascom & Eveleth
Professor at academy .... S. P. Secome
  (A private Monument school)
Presby. Church .... Rev. C. A. Taylor
Saloon .... C. S. Tiner & Co.
Livery Stable ....J. F. Tiner & Co.
Cottage Hotel...................................... Mrs. J. F. Tiner
Blacksmith .... H. Toothaker
General Mdse. .... W. B. Walker
Builder ....J. D. Woodroof
Builder .... George Zimmerman

1881 (Same as the year 1880)

1882
Almost the same as 1880 with a few additions:

Drugs...J. F. Benett
General Mdse. .... R. C. Elliott
Monument Hotel.................................. Mrs. F. R. Ford
Physician .... T. B. Moore
Mayor & Lumber Mill .... L. C. Plummer
Wagon Wheel Maker ....John T. Taylor

1883

Colo. State Business Directory, Denver, Colo.
James Ives & Company, 1883
Monument, Colo. Business Directory

Groceries, etc. .... F. Andrews
Physician and Drugs.............................. Wm. Bonnett
Boots and Shoes.................................... Walter Barnes
Organs and Sewing Machines .... Geo. H. Curtis
Meat Market.. Deal Scott
Millinery and Dry Goods..................... Mrs. Limbach
Monument House.................................. Mrs. C. H. Ford
Blacksmith and Wagon Maker............. John E. Smith
General Mdse. .... W. B. Walker
Livery Stable, Notary, & Real Estate .... A. F. Woodward

1884

Drugs and Physician.............................. W. M. Bonnett
Blacksmith and Wagon Maker............. Moses Chandler
Organ & Sewing Machines................... Geo. H. Curtis
Sewing Machines .... Daniel Davidson
General Mdse. & Cheese Factory........ R. C. Elliott
Boots and Shoes.................................... W. M. Horner
Harness and Saddlery .... H. F. Lee
Postmaster .... W. E. Holbrook
Millinery and Dry Goods..................... Mrs. Limbach
Saloon... Henry Limbach
Monument House.................................. Mrs. H. E. Ford, Prop.
Meat Market.. W. M. Roberts
Blacksmith.. Jno. E. Smith
General Mdse. .... W. B. Walker
Livery Stable, Whsle. potatoes, Notary,
& Real Estate .... A. F. Woodward
Carpenter.. Geo. Zimmerman

1885

Drugs and Physician	W. M. Bonnett
Livery and Feed	A. Borden
Blacksmith and Wagon Maker	Moses Chandler
Organs and Sewing Machines	Geo. H. Curtis
Music Teacher	Mrs. Geo. Curtis
Cheese Factory & General Mdse.	R. C. Elliott
Saloon	Louie Endter
Boots and Shoes	M. N. Harner
Postmaster	W. E. Holbrook
Millinery and Dry Goods	Mrs. Limbach
Monument House	Mrs. Ford, Prop.
Meat Market	Wm. Roberts
Blacksmith	Jno. Smith
Music Teacher	Mrs. J. E. Smith
General Mdse.	W. B. Walker
Whsle. Potatoes, Notary, & Real Est.	A. F. Woodward
Carpenter	Geo. Zimmerman

1886

Register	E. A. Benedict
Physician and Drugs	W. M. Bonnett
Feed Mill	Bennett and Watkins
Dentist	S. E. Bomber
General Mdse. & Cheese Factory	R.C. Elliott
Tailor	Fred Fermchild
Postmaster	W. E. Holbrook
Meat Market	S.S. Hills
Attorneys	Jameyson & Keen
Millinery & Dry Goods	Mrs. H. Limbach
Saloon	Henry Limbach
Monument House	Wm. Younger, Prop.
Livery & Feed	B. F. Roberts
Bakery & Lunch Room	Mrs. Stagman
Blacksmith	John Smith
Music Teacher	Mrs. J. E. Smith
General Mdse.	W. B. Walker

Whsle. Potatoes, Notary, & Real Est . A. F. Woodward
Carpenter .... Geo. Zimmerman

1887
(Almost the same)

1888

Physician and Drugs	W. M. Bonnett
Restaurant and Bakery.........................	W. M. Clark
Whsle. Potato Dealer	T. J. Conway
Groceries and Postmaster...................	J. M. Duffy
Monument House Prop	A. Dunshee
Gen. Mdse.	R. C. Elliott
Blacksmiths..	Fraker and Sailor
Physician	G. W. Fraker
Livery	M. Griffin
Lumber	W. H. Hill and Co.
Justice of the Peace	Wm. E. Holbrook
Meat Market	O. P. Jackson
Attorney	C. Jameyson
Attorney	P. M. Keen
Millinery and Dress Goods	Mrs. Henry Limbach
Saloon	Henry Limbach
Dry Goods and Groceries	Wm. Lierd
Boots and Shoes	E. J. Lawther
Music Teacher	Mrs. Laura Nethers
Jewelry..	F. M. Pauley
Barber	W. H. Shoup
Bakery..	Mrs. Stagman
Blacksmith	John E. Smith
Music Teacher	Mrs. John E. Smith
Dentist..	D. H. Sullivan
Milliner and Dressmaking..................	Mrs. Walker
	& Mrs. McShane

(Town evidently stopped keeping a city directory after 1888)

POST OFFICE

*T*he first post-office in this vicinity was in 1869, and was located on the David McShane ranch. David McShane was the first postmaster. Mail was brought to the office twice a week, if the weather permitted, by hack or saddle horse.

When the D&RG Railway came through Monument the office was moved to the head of Second Street, and Henry Limbach was the second postmaster. In 1878 the Monument office was made a money-order office through the efforts of Henry Limbach.

There was a great amount of money in this part of the country at that time as there were many saw mills located near the town, also excellent potato and grain harvests. People had no other way of sending their money without going to Colorado Springs and Denver.

William Younger was Postmaster for six months when he concluded that he had served under Democratic administration as long as his conscience would allow, and resigned.

In 1869 Dan Holden had a post-office established on his ranch at the head of Bijou Creek, about 5 miles north of Peyton. This office was served by a post route which began at Monument and proceeded via Table Rock, Gomers Mill, Bijou Basin, Big Sandy, and River Bend. Service was twice a week by hack or saddle horse.

On January 26, 1889, when John Duffy was postmaster, it was reported there were 179 call boxes, 26 general delivery, 12 for papers and 16 lock boxes. It was stated at that time there was not a Fourth class office better equipped than the Monument office.

Edgerton was about 8 miles south of Monument. This item was published in the Colorado Springs Republic June 22, 1889. "Edgerton is without a post-office at present from the fact of the old postmaster throwing up the job. C. H. Thompson was appointed several days ago but before his commission he had left the vicinity and gone to parts unknown. The Edgerton people have come to this city for their mail but are circulating a petition for the appointment of another postmaster and is hoped to have a post-office again soon".

Monument office advanced to a third-class office in the 1940's. Lela Hagedorn was Postmaster at this time.

In the early days there was a post-office at Husted, Gwillimville, Springvalley, Eastonville, and Edgerton. Springvalley P. O. discontinued in 1885 and forwarded to Greenland, and Greenland P. O. discontinued in 1958 and forwarded to Larkspur.

From 1869 to 1959 the post-offices were located in stores or private homes. In 1959 it was the first time Monument had its own new building. This building is the first in Monument to be actually owned although on lease by the post-office Department. It was dedicated April 24, 1960 with Lucille Lavelett as postmaster. Up to 1959 the postmasters had to furnish their own boxes. Now the P. O. department furnishes them.

Due to several housing developments on all sides of Monument and the Woodmoor Corporation development just east of the Town, the office has advanced to a second-class office.

New and larger offices were constructed on Front Street in 1975 and again on Third St. in 2000. The Basset Mill post-office which was 8 miles southeast of Monument was established June 15, 1869 and was discontinued Nov. 11, 1893.

The David McShane House.

Site of the McShane Fort & the location of Monument's first Post Office in 1869.

Gwillimville post-office established April 18, 1878 with G. R. Gwiillim as Postmaster. It was discontinued Aug. 27, 1886 and mail transferred to Monument. Then it was re-established April 29, 1887 with David Gwillim as Postmaster. It was discontinued Sept. 29, 1890 and mail transferred to Monument.

POST OFFICE AT MONUMENT COLORADO
ESTABLISHED ON APRIL 8, 1869

POSTMASTERS	DATE OF APPOINT.
David McShane	April 8, 1869
Henry Limbach	March 8, 1871
William E. Holbrook	December 13, 1880
William M. Younger	June 12, 1886
John M. Duffy	December 30, 1886
Mrs. Catherine Duffy	January 9, 1891
Francis W. Bell	September 10, 1896
Mary S. Bell (acting)	November 9, 1910
Mrs. Anna L. Watts	December 14, 1910
Mrs. Ida Betz	October 14, 1914
Mrs. Goldie Simpson	May 1, 1942
Mrs. Lela Hagedorn	September 16, 1942
Wilbur W. Carrothers	August 15, 1949
Lucille R. Lavelett	March 22, 1957
Mrs. Goldie L. Simpson	September 21, 1962
Doris Blickenstaff (Officer in charge)	January 1, 1975
Doris Blickenstaff, Postmaster	April 25, 1975

David McShane
First Postmaster – 1869.

POST OFFICE DEPARTMENT,
CONTRACT OFFICE,
WASHINGTON, *February 7th*, 187*1*.

Ree Feb 27/71

SIR:

To enable the Topographer of this Department to determine, with as much accuracy as possible, the relative positions of Post Offices, so that they may be correctly delineated on its maps, the Postmaster General requests you to fill up the spaces and answer the questions below, and return the same, verified by your signature and dated, under cover to this Office.

Respectfully, &c.

Giles A. Smith

Second Assistant Postmaster General.

To POSTMASTER AT *Monument*
El Paso Co
Colorado

The (P. O. Dept.) name of my office is *Monument*
✳ Its *local name* is *McShanes Ranche*
It is situated in the *North East* quarter of Section No. *15*, in Township *11 South* (north or south), Range *67 west* (east or west), County of *El Paso*, State of *Colorado*

The name of the most prominent *river* near it is *Equidistant Platte & Arkansas*
The name of the nearest *creek* is *Monument*
This office is *40* miles from said river, on the *South of Platte, and north of Arkansas* side of it, and is
¾ miles from said nearest *creek*, on the *East* side of it.
The name of the nearest office on route No. *17037* is *Huntsville*, and its distance is *12* miles, by the traveled road, in a *North* direction from this my office.
The name of the nearest office, *on the same route*, on the other side, is *this is the terminus* and its distance is —— miles in a —— direction from this my office.
The name of the nearest office *off the route* is *Spring valley*, and its distance by the most direct road is *8*, miles in a *East* direction from this my office.
This office is at a distance of *3 miles* from the *proposed* Station of the *Denver & Rio Grande* Railroad, on the *Road* side of the railroad. *west side*
State, under this, the names of all other offices near your office, in different directions from it, and their distances from it by the most direct roads. *Bassetts mill 8 miles S.E.*
Glen Grove 10 miles NW   Colorado City 20 miles South

✳ If the town, village, or site of the Post Office, be known by *another name* than that of the Post Office, state that other name here, that it may be identified on the map of the State (or Territory).

☞ A *diagram* of the township and sections (or, where the land is not so divided, a sketch map), showing the precise location of your office, together with the adjoining Post Offices, towns, or villages, the roads, railroads, and larger streams or creeks, in addition to the above, will be useful, and is desired.—*See diagram blank* accompanying this, to be filled up.)

(Signature of Postmaster.) *David McShane*

(Date.) *Feb 21st 1871*

A form fixing the location of the first post office to be on the McShane ranch just west of the D&RG tracks. David McShane was the first Postmaster. Colorado was still a territory at the time.

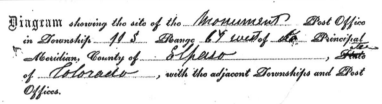

Diagram showing the site of the *Monument* Post Office in Township *11 S* Range *67 west of the* Principal Meridian, County of *El Paso*, State of *Colorado*, with the adjacent Townships and Post Offices.

It is requested that the exact site of the proposed, or existing Post Office, as also the roads to the adjoining offices, and the larger streams or rivers, be marked on this diagram, to be returned as soon as possible to the Post Office Department. If on, or near a railroad, mark the railroad and adjacent station accurately.

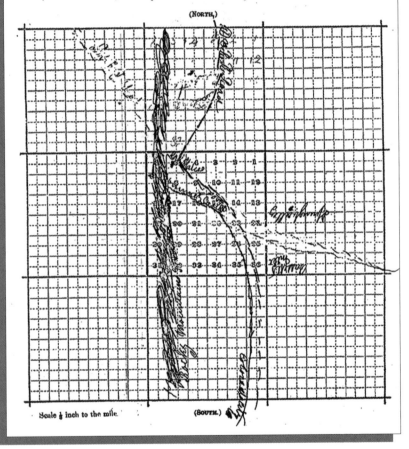

The mapped location of the 2nd post office, drawn by David McShane in 1871, after the D&RG railroad arrived.

Post Office Department,

TOPOGRAPHER'S OFFICE,

Washington, _Aug. 15_, 187_9_.

Sir:

To enable the Topographer of this Department to determine, with as much accuracy as possible, the relative positions of Post Offices, so that they may be correctly delineated on its maps, the Postmaster General requests you to fill up the spaces and answer the questions below, and return the same, verified by your signature and dated, under cover to this Office.

Respectfully, &c.,

W. L. Nicholson
Topographer P. O. Dept.

To Postmaster at _Monument,_
El Paso Co.,
Colo.

The (P. O. Dept.) name of my Office is _Monument_
* Its _local name_ is _Mammut_
It is situated in the _S. E._ ¼ quarter of Section No. _15_, in Township _11_ (north or south), Range _6_ (east or west), County of _El Paso_, State of _Colorado_.

The name of the most prominent _river_ near it is _None_
The name of the nearest _creek_ is _Monument_
This Office is ____ miles from said _river_, on the ____ side of it, and is _One half_ miles from said nearest _creek_, on the _East_ side of it.
The name of the nearest Office on route No. _38118_ is _Greenland_, and its distance is _six_ miles, by the traveled road, in a _East_ direction from this my Office.
The name of the nearest Office, _on the same route_, on the other side, is ____ and its distance is ____ miles in a ____ direction from this my Office.
The name of the nearest Office _off the route_ is _Easton_, and its distance by the most direct road is _12_ miles in a _South Easterly_ direction from this my Office.
This Office is at a distance of _500 ft_ from the _or so_ Station of the _Denver & Rio Grande_ Railroad, on the _East_ side of the railroad.

State, under this, the names of all other Offices near your Office, in different directions from it, and their distances from it by the most direct roads.

* If the town, village, or site of the Post Office, be known by another name than that of the Post Office, state that other name here, that it may be identified on the map of the State (or Territory).

☞ A diagram of the township and sections (or, where the land is not so divided, a sketch map,) showing the precise location of your Office, together with the adjoining Post Offices, towns, or villages, the roads, railroads, and larger streams or creeks, in addition to the above, will be useful, and is desired.—(See diagram blank accompanying this, to be filled up.)

(Signature of Postmaster.) _Henry Limbach_

(Date.) _Sept 27 1879_

When the D&RG came through, the location of the post office moved from the McShane ranch to Second St. Henry Limbach was the second postmaster taking office in 1871.

{ 35 }

CEMETERY

*I*n 1886 Charles R. Bissell conveyed to the Town of Monument a five-acre tract of land that had been used as a cemetery since 1871. The deed was dated May 28, 1886 and recorded the same day in Book 50, page 237. In 1889 it was surveyed and platted and recorded in Plat Book 28, page 28. At this time a newspaper correspondent wrote from Monument "Hither-to the dead were buried indiscriminately, no one having a lot and families have consequently become badly mixed. Here-after a certain sum will be required for each lot and the money derived therefrom will be used for the improvement of cemetery". At that time Council fixed the price of lots at $10.00 each and hired a sexton at $5.00 a year to take care of the cemetery. In the 1920's J. A. Bougher donated ground on the east Side of the cemetery to Town for more plots. My grandfather, John Olfs, planted the first four pine trees in the cemetery. Grandfather claimed to be an atheist. His first grandchild, whom he loved dearly, died at the age of 2 ½ years. Grandfather dug up four trees from his homestead, which was where the Woodmoor Barn is in 2004. He planted them at the corners of the grave and said "If these four trees grow I'll know there is a God in Heaven, and little Harry is in Heaven". Little was known about transplanting trees in those days, but all four trees grew and are big trees now. Mrs. Hattie E. Thompson Neese was the first person buried in the cemetery. In 1920 with Mrs. Ballou as chairman and help of the people in the community, water pipes were laid and a windmill used to pump water into a tank, which supplied water throughout the cemetery. Vandal's shot holes in the tank, the windmill was torn down, and the pipes are all rusted now.

POOL HALL

I n 1917 and 1918 Bob Burrell operated a pool hall on the east side of Front Street, which was the former Limbach saloon.

The United States entered World War I on the Allied side in the spring of 1917. It is not known why the Burrell Pool Hall only stayed in business for two years. Possibly there was a shortage of young men wanting to play the game. Note the college pennants in the rear of the photograph. The identity of the young man on the left is unknown. The gentleman wearing the cap in the right-foreground is Jeff Pribble.

MONUMENT HOTEL

*T*he Monument Hotel was considered one of the finest for complete rest and relaxation when it was built in 1870. It was owned and operated by Col. and Mrs. Ford. It had 19 sleeping rooms all furnished and carpeted in the early style. It had an elegant parlor, office, and adjoining reading room. Col. and Mrs. Ford came to Monument from Maine. Mrs. Ford supervised the dining room and her meals were of the finest. The windows and veranda to the west afforded a beautiful view of the mountains and invalids desiring a quiet, comfortable home found the hotel a lovely place to stay. The charges were $2.00 a day with generous reductions by the week. Others who operated the hotel were Dr. and Mrs. Ballou, and Dr. and Mrs. Rupp, and Mr. and Mrs. Roy Petrie. Other hotels in town were the Park Hotel, Ironside, and Grand Arm.

The Monument Hotel located on Front Street – ca 1870.

Colonel & Mrs. Ford founded the Monument Hotel.
Rates were $2.00 per day with board extra.

Monument Hotel, W-side, with Margaret Rupp and one of
Dr. Rupp's fine trotting horses.

MONUMENT ACADEMY

O n the 4th of November 1878, a private school opened in Monument with 15 students and increased to 25. The reason for this school was to give students instructions in a more advanced range than was taught in the District's school. The trustees of this school were Chas. A. Taylor, R. J. Gwillim, J. F. Wood, and A. T. Blachly. Mr. Chas. Taylor was the principal with W. N. Holbrook and Mrs. J. T. Blachly, assistants. The instruction was under the control of the Presbyterian denomination, and it was to prepare the students for the Colorado Springs College. Board was $4.00 per week and the rates of tuition for English branches $6.00 per quarter and $7.00 for mathematics. This academy was in operation for just a few years and apparently closed for lack of funds.

The 2nd Monument School built – ca 1880 had three rooms. The school was just north of Dirty Women Gulch.

PUBLIC SCHOOL

*T*he first school was a log building built where the Denver & Rio Grande tracks are now. When the railroad was built in 1870 the school was moved just north of the Dirty Woman Gulch. In the 1880's a three-room white frame building was built. The first eight grades were taught. The third room was not used in this building for several years, only as a playroom in cold weather.

Two teachers were hired; one for grades one to four, and one for grades fifth to the eighth. In 1917 a third teacher was obtained and the first two years of high school taught. In 1917 and 1918 El Paso County's superintendent of schools, Inez Johnson Lewis, knew more boys and girls should have a high school education. She began to talk and work for the consolidation of the small one-room schools. Her efforts and hard work became a reality and in the fall of 1920 the new consolidated school opened and was named after her, Inez Johnson Lewis. The districts that consolidated were: Pring, 3 miles south of Monument; Husted, 6 miles south; Stout, which was east of Husted; Elton, and Gwillimville east of Monument. The first graduating class had only one graduate, Bernice Ingersol. In 1922 there were two; Ethel Dwyer and Blanche Clark. In 1923 there were just two; Elizabeth Hunt and Ralph Gelvin. Later Columbine District near the Douglas County line consolidated with Monument. Lewis consolidated district number at that time was No.5. For several years Palmer Lake paid tuition for their high school students to come to Monument.

In the 1930's Palmer Lake voted to consolidate with Lewis Consolidated School. Palmer Lake's district number was 33 so they combined 5 and 33 and it became District 38 and named it Lewis Palmer. Palmer Lake maintained its grade school.

In the 1950's Black Forest consolidated with Monument and a new grade school built in the Forest, and a new high school in Monument. Black Forest remained in Monument District until the Academy built their high school, then they withdrew from District 38 and went to District 20. The original white frame school was for several years used as a garage and bus maintenance shop. Floyd Bellinger was in charge of this shop for several years. It was torn down in 1970 and a new administration building built on the grounds. Due to the population increase on all sides of Monument, a new Middle School has been built east of town. It is one of the finest and up-to-date schools in the county and state.

Mr. John L. Pound was the first Superintendent of the new consolidated school in 1920. Inez Johnson Lewis became an accredited high school while Donald McKay was Superintendent in 1922. He was a very progressive superintendent. Although the school had all credentials to become an accredited high school, except it had no electricity, because Monument had no electricity at that time. Mr. McKay was influential in having the School Board wire for electricity and it passed for accreditation. For several years Coleman gaslights were hung from the ceilings for light. The school did not have a gym until 1927 when the District was financially able to build one on the west side of the school.

The School Board members in 1920 and 1921 were E. J. James, W. E. Higby, and W. W. Doughty. The first annual was dedicated to them.

In 1922 the Faculty members were: Principal and Mathematics, Donald McKay; Wilbur Fulker, Manual Training; Myrtie Bridges, Music and Penmanship; Miss Ruth Rose, 4th and 5th grades; Bessie Hagen, English, History, Art; Junior High. Miss Ruth Hanna, 2nd and 3rd grades; Betty MacKay, Domestic Art; Mrs. Josephine Mays, English, History, and Latin; Gladys Crissey, 1st grade and kindergarten.

The "Inez Johnson Lewis", Consolidated School – 1923.
" **Big Red** "

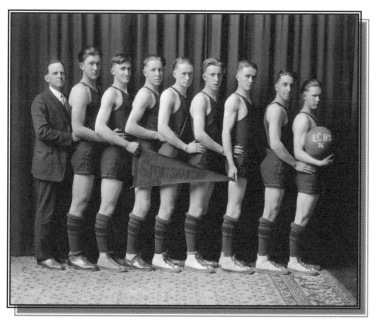

Basketball team of Lewis Consolidated High School – 1925-26.

Monument School
8th Grade
1925-26

Jack Friendly, Lloyd Travis, Harry Horner, David Higby
Juanita Brown, Violet Carlson, May Murr
Leah Barnhart, Fern Friendly, Ruby McCarty, Lela Van Fleet

{ 44 }

Monument School – 1916 – Grades 1 - 8

Bottom Row from Left

Barney McShane, Grant Boling, John Barnhardt, Loren Cale, Charles Smelsen, Harry Barnhardt, Homer Ganes, Harold Garrett, Neil Shields, William Watts, Rosamond Barnhardt, Lincoln Romack, Mildred Hagedorn, Chester Boling

Second Row

Fred Millwright, Lavonia Boling, Francis Smelser, Ed Cole, Hazel Barnhardt, Eva Judd, Stoddard Millwright, Everett Ganes, Bradford Harlin, Frank Barnhardt, Jessie Clark, Marie Judd, Paul Garrett, Winston Kirton, Sarah Boling, Lily Smelsen

Third Row

Lela Dolan, Margaret Olfs, Katherine Romack, Clara Clark, Pauline Romack, Lucille Hagedorn, Frances Garrett, Gertrude Olfs, Hazel Miller (Teacher Grades 1 – 4)

Back Row

Gladys Clark, Norma Watts, Blanche Clark, Phillip McShane, Elizabeth Whalen, Gladys Ganes, Elsie Romack, Esther Stamm, Ressionell Harlin, P.A. Kirton (Grades 5 – 8)

DIRTY WOMAN GULCH

*D*irty Woman Gulch as it was named in the 1870's and later called Dirty Woman Creek, is the first creek crossed when entering Monument from the south. It is south of the Monument School and is a branch of the Monument Creek. In the 1870's the school was built near the gulch. Near the stream lived a woman in a shack. The woman kept goats, chickens, cats, dogs, and other animals and did not keep it or herself very clean, so in speaking, the kids called it Dirty Woman Gulch and still is known by that name.

From the diary of Mrs. Byron N. Sanford, 12/27/1861

"Last night we stopped at what is called 'Dirty Woman's Ranch' and really it could have no more appropriate name. Minnie and I go into houses and cook meals when we can. As we entered the door of this place the woman was pelting something with a broomstick. A young pig had wandered into the kitchen and got his head fast in the cream jar. It fitted pretty close and in frantic efforts to get loose, rolled over and over the floor, while the youngsters who swarmed, it seemed, scampered under the beds as the mother pounded and yelled until, at last, jar and pig rolled out into the yard. We made our coffee and drank it with a meager lunch, deciding we had scant time to cook. We gave the youngsters some cookies as they gaped at us in wonder, paid the 'Dirty Woman' for her trouble and returned to camp.

POTATOES

*T*he Divide potatoes were known as the best potatoes in the country. It was the chief industry. In 1877 the greatest number of potatoes raised to the acre was 25,000 pounds by Paton Wilson. The average numbers of pounds were from 4 to 6 thousand per acre. In 1875 potatoes sold for 75 cents a hundred. One potato would weigh 31/4 pounds with different varieties running up to 27 inches in marketable condition to the vine. At potato harvest time it wasn't uncommon to see 60 wagon loads of potatoes in a day coming from Table Rock and Gwillimville areas to be stored in Walker's large potato cellar or to be shipped out. At first Denver and Colorado Springs were the only markets for the Divide potatoes, but Monument soon became a permanent shipping point. The first shipper was Posey and Wingate in 1873. Chas. Tiner filled the first government contract in 1881. In that year Divide potatoes first entered into competition with other parts of the state. In 1879 F. S. Millwright, who lived 6 miles east of Monument, raised the champion potatoes. They were dry land potatoes and 6 acres yielded 20 to 25 tons. In the 1920's Lou Steppler, whose ranch was in the Table Rock area was known as "Divide Potato King". In 1889 Monument sent out 380 (*Some accounts put the number of railcar loads at 2,000.*) cars of potatoes to Kansas, Texas, New Mexico, and Arizona. Potato Bake Day was always a great event. It was always about the 10th of October after the harvest. It was a day of fun and enjoyment, also good advertising for Monument potatoes. Special trains were run that day to bring people to the Bake. On Oct. 11, 1890 the Colorado Springs Herald wrote the following: "Yesterday was a big day for Monument for the annual Potato Bake. Fully 1500 people came from all parts near and far to enjoy the hospitality. The Mt. Herman band furnished music for the occasion. The menu was two roast beefs, four roast sheep, two roast hogs, and fifty bushels of potatoes, plenty of home-made bread, butter, cakes, pies, and coffee." All this was free. Farmers and merchants donated everything, and a committee of men dug the pits, baked the potatoes, and roasted the meat. It was held west of the Rio Grande tracks and east of Monument Lake. In the afternoon there were horseshoe pitching, tugs of war, and a baseball game. At night a dance in the Walker Hall finished the day. A blight, the "psyllid yellows," beginning in 1895 caused by insects common on wild rose bushes put an end to the big potato crops.

A Monument grown, 3 lb. Spud – ca 1908.

10/2/1886 – From the Monument Register – J. D. Tourtelotte, of Greenland is bringing in his potatoes with four-horse teams, 4,000 pounds to the load. He reports his crops better than he has ever raised on the Divide. He had thirteen acres in last year, and this year he has about thirty. He has all hands at work digging and hauling to market while the price is up. His other crops he says are very good. Mr. Tourtelotte is one of the Divide's most prosperous farmers and attends closely and carefully to his business.

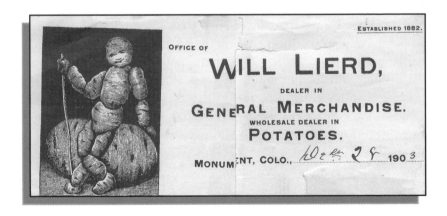

"Dry Land" potato farming.

The Monument "Potato Bake" – ca 1892.
Photos courtesy of the Colorado Springs Pioneers Museum

{ 49 }

THRESHING MACHINES

*I*n the early years this area had three threshing machines, steam engines and crews owned by Albert McShane and son, Dave; Hugo Schubarth and sons, Charlie and Guy; and L. H. Gaunt and son, Roy. Earl Thompson operated the engine for L. H. Gaunt. Threshing day was a big exciting, happy, hard-working time for the entire family.

The women always prepared the meals with about 16 extra men to cook for. The engineer would back the grain separator between the large stacks of grain with a big criss-cross belt running all the way to the engine. The men climbed to the top of the big grain stacks and pitched the grain bundles into one end of the separator. Grain would come out of one spout, and weed seed from another, which was saved and soaked in skim milk and fed to the pigs. The grain spout had a gauge that the farmer watched closely that told him how many bushels his grain crop was yielding. The straw was used for bedding for livestock and sometimes stuffed in large ticks for youngsters to sleep on. Fresh new straw was a treat to sleep on. Grain was hauled to Monument Market in lumber wagons. If the roads were soft and muddy it would take eight horses to pull the wagon piled high with sacks of grain and the driver of the teams on top.

COFFINS, UNDERTAKERS

*T*hree general stores sold coffins. They were owned by Will Lierd, Jno. E. Smith, and J. F. Roth. They were also undertakers. Mrs. Bertha Curry was Monument's last undertaker about 1916. She would go to the home of the deceased and lay the body out in the home. A bedroom was closed off for this purpose. In the summer-time tubs were filled with ice and set on the floor under the bodies until the funeral.

Some of the family and friends would sit up all night with the body. Mr. Lierd, a very honest man, always paid his debts and expected everyone else to do the same. He sold a coffin to a party and they would not pay so he started to sue. They finally came to pay for the coffin, $50.00; they brought the money all in pennies and made him count it out. From then on he was known as "Penny Lierd".

Charlie Schubarth with Engine & Thresher – 1916.

Will "Penny" Lierd, Fred Sailor, & A. Curry in Lierd's Store.

CROPS

O ther crops raised to sell and feed stock were Rye, Oats, and Corn. In 1888 H. B. Walker claimed to have the finest field of oats in the country. The stand of the oat field was 4-1/2 feet high with well-filled heads, with a yield of 40 or 45 bushels per acre. O. P. Jackson had 100 acres of corn. In 1889 Rye was reported to be 3 feet high and excellent yield per acre. In 1878 it was estimated that there were 75,000 to 100,000 bushels of grain to be ground in the Monument vicinity. In 1890 Monument was the main shipping point on the D&RG railroad. One year, Monument shipped out 380 cars of potatoes, 100 cars of lumber, 75 cars of cordwood. And 16 cars filled with grains. Cutting and baling hay and straw was done extensively each year.

In 1881, potato diggers were in high demand. Farmers were paying $1.75 per day and board.

SAWMILLS

T he Bassett Mill was 8 miles southeast of Monument in 1875, there was also a post-office there. Calvin Husted had a mill 6 miles south of Monument. Husted Station was named for him. When the Air Academy came in, it took all the land where east and west Husted Stations were once busy little places. In 1875 ties were being cut on top of Mt. Herman and slid down the mountain. Some of the big slides on the Mountain can still be seen. Tomlinson Bros. and Ruggles were getting them down at the rate of 100 a day. Henry Limbach had 15,000 ties upon the track the 1st of May 1875. The last sawmill in this area was owned and operated by Bernie Frank in the 1950's; this was 1-½ miles north of Monument.

Galley's Hay Ranch, located in the Monument area – ca 1903.

The Guire Ranch – ca 1895.
Photos courtesy of the Colorado Springs Pioneers Museum

Mr. Brown and his son William Jr. are cutting and binding grain on their ranch about six miles east of Monument.

Albert McShane & son Dave with their steam engine – ca 1915.

The Pettigrew Ranch & Home, Rube Pribble standing – ca 1900.
Rube would later shoot-kill his best friend at Limbach's Saloon.

Hauling Potatoes to Monument for shipment – ca 1890.

SALOONS AND MURDERS

M onument always had its saloons and whiskey men. Two murders were committed in the Limbach saloon. A feud between Daniel Davidson and Francis Brown developed over a cattle transaction; each accused the other of stealing cattle. On Oct. 21, 1876 they met in the saloon and exchanged words. Davidson drew his pistol and shot Brown twice. Brown died almost instantly. He is buried in the Monument Cemetery, and his stone reads: "He was killed". A trial was held in February 1877. The jury found Davidson guilty. His lawyers obtained a writ of supersedeas and he was released on a bond of $5,000.00. Almost three years of litigation followed. The second trial began Feb. 13, 1880 and on February 21 Davidson was found not guilty. He was elected to the Town Board in 1881 and Davidson was the promoter of the ordinance passed prohibiting the shooting of fire-arms in town, and increasing liquor licenses to $300.00 a year.

The second murder committed in a saloon was a feud between Rube Pribble and Mr. Neff. Mr. Pribble accused Neff of stealing a plow from him. Mr. Pribble shot and killed Neff. On Sunday morning when he was shown Neff's body, his only words were "I have killed my best friend". Pribble was found guilty and sentenced to life in the penitentiary. On second trial it was brought out Neff had not stolen the plow but a third party had, and hid it in a barn. Pribble then was sentenced to 25 years, but died of pneumonia in a short time.

The license fee to sell liquor in 1897 was $500.00. The Town had a very active W. C. T. U. organization (Women's Christian Temperance Union). There were always battles going on between Temperance folks and Whiskey men. The Whiskey men usually won every town election, except in April 1896. That year Ordinance No. 33 was passed prohibiting selling liquor in town.

The W. C. T. U. folks sent a thank you resolution to Board Members to be written upon the minutes. Evidently the Whiskey men gave the Temperance a bad time for one-by-one Temperance resigned until Whiskey got power again and Ordinance No. 36 repealed Ordinance No. 33 and saloons were wide open again. One W. C. T. U. lady would gather up the whiskey bottles and hang them by the neck on her fence and put up a sign "I am hanging John Barley Corn".

Burrell's Billiard Hall formerly
Limbach's Saloon & Barbershop – ca 1917.

"Frontier Justice" was swift, but not always sure.

Two men were shot and killed, in separate incidents, in this saloon located on Front St. next to the Walker Bldg, on the right. At least one of the men killed was innocent of any wrongdoing.

NO CHANCE FOR CRIMINALS

*T*he Pioneers had their own method for taking care of criminals. In November 1867 a young homesteader was found murdered in his cabin on Plum Creek, south of Castle Rock. Two strange men had been seen going south on the creek and the neighbors became suspicious and a posse was soon formed. It was learned the suspects had spent the night at the home of Dan Hopkins about two miles north of Palmer Lake. Hopkins joined the posse and they soon overtook the criminals near Monument. After starting on the return trip and about a mile north of Palmer Lake one of the men became very abusive so the posse halted in a pine grove and strung him up. A few hours later the posse reached a gulch about a mile north of Castle Rock, held a trial, and the second prisoner was also hanged.

Dan Hopkins and other members of the Hopkins family are buried in the Monument Cemetery.

MONUMENT STATE BANK

*M*elvin Olson who worked in the bank at the time it opened gave the history of Monument State Bank to me.

The bank started to organize in 1916. The directors and stockholders were W. E. Higby, Dr. Wm. McConnell, Charles Allis, and A. M. Staley, cashier. The directors purchased the stone building on the corner of Front and Second Street from W. B. Walker estate. The bank opened Sept. 1917. In six months A. M. Staley sold his shares to Ralph E. Walker and he and Florence Rupp Glendening operated the bank until Mr. Walker sold to Clyde Taylor. Melvin Olson worked for Clyde Taylor until June 1920. Then Harry Taylor, Clyde's son, worked in the bank. Some time in the 1920's W. E. Higby and Dr. McConnell sold their holdings to a Mr. Snowden. Joy Taylor, Clyde's brother; Harry Taylor; and Mr. Snowden operated the bank until 1924 at which time the bank closed its doors.

The bank building is shown on page 12.

Checks from the Monument State Bank.

DOCTORS AND DRUG STORES

*T*he first drug store was operated by A. Trew Blachly and his brother, Frank, was the first doctor in 1875. Other doctors through the years were Dr. Robertson; Henry Cook (1878); H. Eddy (1880); Wm. Bonnett (1883); T. B. Moor (1882); S. E. Bomber, a dentist (1886); Dr. Ballou in the 1880's; Dr. Wm. McConnell (1895); Dr. Rupp (1895); Dr. D. H. Sullivan, a dentist; Dr. Close (1918); Dr. Meyers; Dr. McDaniels; and Dr. Schlawig, a dentist.

Alexander Boston McConnell brought his family to Colorado in 1876 and bought land at Table Rock, ten miles east of Monument. William McConnell finished the eighth grade at Table Rock, went to Denver to Warren Academy for secondary school. He got his A. B. degree in 1887 and M. A. in Pharmacology, graduated Medical School in 1893. He interned in St. Louis and practiced there one year, then located in Monument in 1895. Lucy Anne Pring sprained her ankle one-day in 1897 and was taken to Dr. McConnell for treatment-they were married in 1898. Dr. McConnell was appointed railway physician for both Santa Fe and D&RG railroads. This covered all employees between Castle Rock and Husted. Dr. McConnell's home and office was on Second Street across from the Town Hall. Dr. McConnell and his wife were civic-minded people. He was one of the main supporters of the Monument baseball team. Mrs. McConnell was a leader in the Temperance movement.

John Pring and family came to Colorado in 1876 and bought land south of Monument. Pring Station was named after him; it was just three miles south of town.

Dr. and Mrs. Rupp came to Monument in the 1890's from Illinois. He came to Colorado to seek relief from asthma. He had his first office in the south end of town on Front Street, which was called "five points". He later bought the Monument

Hotel and had his doctor's office there. He was a conscientious doctor. He never sent a bill to his patients, if his patients could pay him they would, and he said he lost very little of his fees. He had a pair of fast trotters, and a third he drove single. He gave them the best of care and feed. He would not have an automobile, even after they became common. He said his trotters could make better time over those country roads. Dr. Rupp was also town treasurer and water commissioner for many years. He died at the age of 74 and is buried in the Monument Cemetery.

Dr. T. H. Close came to Monument in 1917. He was a fine doctor during the 'flu epidemic in 1918 and 1919, he never lost a patient. He and his wife were good, civic-minded people. They had one son, Harland, who also became a doctor.

Dr. Francis McConnell-Mills   Dr. William McConnell

Dr. F. Mills became a famed toxicologist in Denver Co. The laboratory tests she performed provided the necessary evidence to convict many killers. She was part of the Crime Scene Investigation (CSI) teams of her day.

The photo of Dr. W. McConnell was taken at his medical school graduation.

BLACKSMITHS, LIVERY STABLES, AND WAGON WHEEL MAKERS

M onument always had good blacksmiths and they were kept busy sharpening plow shares, shoeing horses, tightening the wagon wheel rims, and making wagon wheels.

Other blacksmiths not mentioned in the Town Directory were VanDyne, Dennis Whalen, Harry Dalton, Chas. P. Clark, and Clarence Croft. The last blacksmith was George Tucker who had his shop on the corner of Third Street and Beacon Light Road. The livery stables were kept busy hauling supplies that were shipped in by rail to the General Merchandise stores, and renting horses and buggies to tourists.

The Elliott's were an industrious couple owning several businesses in Monument. Please note the name 'Studebaker Wagons' just above the door. Studebaker would soon turn to building automobiles. These liveries were the full service transportation centers of the time – ca 1892.

THE D&RG AND SANTA FE RAILROADS

*T*he D&RG was Monument's first railroad in 1871; the first train came through Jan. 1, 1872. The Town granted the Santa Fe a right-of-way in 1887 and trains started through in 1892. There were two depots in Monument; one at Pring Station; and two at Husted. Every three miles both railroads had section crews to maintain the tracks. Each section employed a section boss and a crew of several men. DeLos Barnhardt was the Santa Fe section boss for many years. The men worked for 40 cents an hour, 6 days a week. Each depot had an agent and two trick (8 hour shift) operators. E. W. Hunt was the Santa Fe agent for many years, and Gladys Clark was a trick operator. The last agent for the Santa Fe was W. N. Willis. Pearl Archer was an operator on the D&RG at Monument and Husted for many years. Roy Deffenbaugh was a long-time agent on the D&RG. Both railroads had stockyards. In the fall when the farmers shipped their cattle to market it was a busy time for the entire town. Some Farmers had their cattle on the government range all summer. Seeing the men driving their cattle off the range and checking the brands was an interesting event to watch. Several days before the ranchers wanted to ship their cattle; the railroad would spot the cattle cars on the siding. Almost all the cattlemen would ship out the same day. Seeing several hundred head of cattle being driven by the men on their good well trained horses, through town to the yards was an exciting and interesting day. The next day the switch engine came and the cattle were loaded in the cars. Cattle shipping day was a busy eventful time for farmers and the town's people. When the automatic block (green, yellow, and red) signals telling the train engineer to proceed, proceed-w/caution or stop) became available in the 1940's many of the depots were no longer needed and were closed. A block was a mile or more of track and a manually operated block-signal was located at the depot. A red signal would be given as a train passed the first block, located at the depot. As the train passed the 2nd block the signal would change to yellow and so on.

Both depots remained open for a time but were closed then moved close to Highway 105 and converted into restaurants about 1949. Later they were torn down and burned. For several years all Northbound trains ran on the Santa Fe, and Southbound on the D&RG. In September 1974 Santa Fe tracks were no longer used and D&RG tracks now handle the north and Southbound freight. The Santa Fe tracks were torn out in November 1974. Coal trains are now the most common traffic.

Monument D&RG station agent Harry S. Maddox (R) – ca 1910.
Photo courtesy of Ted Colley.

A Santa Fe, mixed freight train northbound, 1930.

The D&RG depot – ca 1947.

The D&RG depot - ca 1918.

Do note the "Block" semaphore signal located at the upper right hand of the photo. The station agent would manually place the semaphore at the correct angle. The semaphore had three colored lenses being green, yellow, and red to indicate whether the train engineer should proceed, slow, or stop respectively.

In the photo, the signal is set at the angle and color indicating that the train should stop.

Monument, 1894. The Walker Bldg. on 2nd St. (L-C) is followed by the Monument and Park Hotels to the right.

Santa Fe Railroad depot, W. N. Willis agent – ca 1947.

The Santa Fe underpass once located just east of Washington St. on hwy 105. John Bovard & Clarence Lavelett are preparing the roadbed for paving in 1927. The new highway opened in 1928.

(Addendum: See page 131 for photographs of the Santa Fe train wreck of July, 1895.)

{ 67 }

BUTCHER SHOPS

C has. Allis had a butcher shop on the corner of Second and Washington Streets in the 1890's. Later this place became a restaurant operated by Van Fimple. George Betz and John Boling operated a meat market and delivered meat by wagon for several years. There was Pauls Meat Market operated by Paul Close and Paul Valentine. When meat was delivered by wagon, the back of the wagon was closed in, with hooks to hang meat on, a meat block, and scales. In the summer-time large tubs were filled with ice to keep the meat cold. Butchers would make a trip twice a week to Palmer Lake, and to people as far east as Table Rock. Butchers always came back with empty wagons. The floor of the butcher shop always had about three inches of clean sawdust to keep the dust down.

Once a week the floor was cleaned and new saw dust shavings put on the floor again. Higby Mercantile had a butcher shop in the back of the store, and was noted for having the best meat in the area.

The Betz Meat Market, 65 Second St. – ca 1910.

Mr. Turner & Mark Schubarth delivering to the "Pines"
Cottage located in the Glen of Palmer Lake, 1913.

George Betz, center, and his chain drive delivery truck, the first
in Monument – ca 1914. Note the hard-rubber 'tires.'

PARKS

*I*n 1883 Chas. Adams donated block 2, west of Front Street to the Town for a park. Monument minutes state that the Town Board in behalf of the Town extended him a letter of thanks for his generous gift. Trees were planted in 1884, and the land seeded to grass in 1885 by Henry Limbach. The park is now named "Limbach Park". The status of this land is in question as of mid 2004 in that about one-half of this park, to the south, is owned by the railroad. Negotiations are in progress to acquire this land permanently for the town.

In the late 1960's the Town filed a claim on a tract of land for a park north of Third Street and west of Beacon Light Road. This land from the time of incorporation of Town had been known as "No Man's Land". It is now named in honor of the Monument historian and the original author of this book, "Lucille Lavelett."

A third park was added in 1979 at "Dirty Woman Creek." The park bears that name dating back to 1861.

FIRST TELEPHONES & TELEGRAPH

*A*n ordinance granting certain privileges to the Colorado Telephone Company in the Town of Monument was approved on the 23rd of June 1896 when J. E. Smith was Mayor.

Monument had the only Western telegraph office between Denver and Colorado Springs in 1875.

WOODMAN HALL

*T*he Monument Woodman of the World Camp organized in July 1896. It was known as Camp 302. The W. O. W. built their hall on the south side of Second Street. It was a thriving organization until 1929 when all members transferred to Camp No.5 in Colorado Springs. W. O. W. sold the hall to W. E. Higby in which he used to store hay and farm machinery. In 1941, when Nancy Williams was president of the Homemakers' Club, Mr. Higby gave the building to the Homemakers' organization. The hall had deteriorated and needed a lot of repair work, but the entire community helped to make it a nice building. In 1965 the club deeded the building to the Town with the understanding that the Club could have use of the building for club meetings at no charge. Each year improvements have been made to the hall, and in 1974 it was the best Town Hall Monument had owned until the current Hall was built in 1980.

In 1900 the Grand Army had a hall at the head of First Street. In the 1880's Monument had a District Court, and on its seal was number 1248.

The Woodman Hall was torn down and replaced by the current Town Hall in 1980.

DOYLE ICE & STORAGE COMPANY

*F*red Lewis and his wife, Myrtle McKee Lewis, who now live in Grand Junction, Colorado, gave this history of the ice plant to me. Fred Lewis is the brother-in-law of the late W. E. Doyle. Mrs. Lewis was a teacher in the Lewis Consolidated School in 1923. Fred Lewis went to work for Doyle in 1910. He was timekeeper and foreman until 1927.

In 1901 Doyle and Thomas Hanks leased the lake known then as the State Reservoir. Wm. Doyle owned the land on the east Side of the lake. They built the original icehouse with a short chute to carry the ice from the lake. It was known as "Hanks and Doyle Ice Company". The first ice plant was built of native lumber from a sawmill located in the Black Forest and owned by J. W. Higby.

Harvesting ice at that time was done by men and horses. The power for conveying the ice up into the houses was supplied by horses. The ice harvest began about the middle of December and the cakes of ice were 24 inches thick after being planed. 20,000 to 30,000 tons were harvested. 4,000 tons were stored in the houses and the balance shipped to Pueblo and Denver.

In 1909 Doyle bought out Hanks and constructed five new houses, each with a conveyor chain powered by a threshing machine engine steamer, owned and operated by Hugo and Charlie Schubarth. A spur railroad track was put in to load ice directly into the railroad cars.

On Dec. 31, 1909 a 75 to 100 mile per-hour West wind completely demolished the icehouses on the day before they were to start the harvest. That was a bad financial loss for Doyle, also for the men who planned to work that winter. The houses were rebuilt.

Forty to fifty men and 8 teams of horses were employed in the winter for 25 to 30 days to pack ice in the houses and to ship to Denver and Pueblo, Colorado. Each layer of ice cakes in the houses were covered and packed in about 12 inches of sawdust. In the summer the Ice Company employed 15 to 20 men for 30 to 40 days shipping ice.

The wages in those days were 40 cents per hour for men working ten hours a day, 7 days a week. Men were paid $2.00 a day for their team of horses. In 1920 Doyle replaced the horse-drawn plows for cutting ice with two gasoline powered plows, which took the place of six horses and ten men. In ice harvest days, the winters were COLD! From the first of November Monument could always plan on the weather to range from 10 to 20 below zero every night until the first of February and the ground completely covered with snow all winter. The lake would freeze over and stay frozen. At night, to keep the channel from freezing over, a man worked to bring in a float of ice every hour. Later a man used a rowboat to keep the channel open. At the water box, which was at the beginning of the chute, men used a steel spud tool with sharp prongs on one end, cutting the floats of ice into cakes and pushing them up to the chute with pike poles.

W. E. Doyle had a 20-year contract with the American Refrigerated Transit. In the early 1930's Monument began to have warm and open winters. The lawyer failed to put a clause in the contract "If due to weather conditions the ice crop failed, contract would not be fulfilled" so Doyle had to forfeit several thousand dollars, which broke him and forced him to sell to VanDiest. On Nov. 10, 1932 an agreement was made with the A. R. T. to take over the entire operation. The railroad spur owned by the Ice Company was assigned in 1936 to the A. R. T. for other debts.

In 1943 a terrific West wind once again swept over the mountains and blew down the icehouses. Heavy timbers and planks tore through Monument like a hurricane. One 2x4 from the icehouse was embedded in the sidewall of a home on Second Street. When the Doyle Ice Company was a good flourishing business Mr. Doyle and Fred Lewis, without borrowed funds, built the beautiful home east of the lake. Every store, hotel, restaurant, and some homes had their own ice houses where the cakes of ice were packed in saw dust that kept all summer.

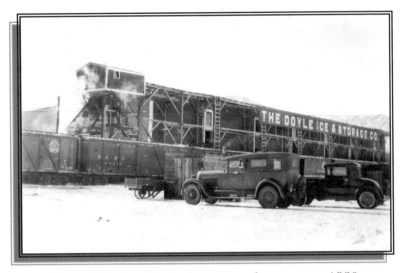

One of the five Doyle ice storage houses – ca 1930.

Prior to powered saws, the ice was grooved in a parallel block pattern to a depth 3 inches from the bottom, with a series of horse drawn grooving knives. The gasoline powered saw would replace six horses and ten men in performing this task – ca 1910.

The Doyle Ice Harvest was a major employer in the winter.

Marking the cuts (upper) and sawing the grooves – ca 1921.

"Spudding" cakes of ice from the ice-float at the water box prior to conveying the cakes to the storage house – ca 1915.

Ice being loaded into boxcars for use in food transport by rail, truck, or for consumption – ca 1925.

Mr. & Mrs. Doyle at the peak of their business – ca 1925.

Throughout WW II the uniquely American ice harvest played a
major role in keeping food fresh for distribution and cutting
waste. The ice harvest in Monument ceased in 1943.

NEWSPAPERS

*T*he Mentor was Monument's first newspaper, established by A. T. Blachly in 1878. The Mentor discontinued publication in 1880. In March 1880 G. B. Armstrong and John Guire published the Monument Journal. The next paper was the El Paso County Register edited and published by E. A. Benedict from Oct. 1885 to July 1889. After Benedict left town the Register was edited by Frank L. Crampton for a few months and was discontinued about the end of 1889. In 1890 the "Monument Recorder" was edited by Mrs. C. E. Duffy and was mentioned by contemporaries as late as October of that year. In the meantime the Monument Messenger had been started. The Council approved a bill from this paper on June 2, 1890.

The Messenger lasted until 1911, and had several editors including W. S. Neal, O. H. Whittier, C. D. Ford, and C. A. Bent.

In the 1950's "Preacher Sam" who lived in a house by the Monument Lake published the Lake View Press. This was edited only a few months. Stanley Johnson edited the Columbine Herald in the 1950's. In the 1960's Monument, Palmer Lake News, which later included the Woodmoor News was edited and printed by George Kobolt of Castle Rock, Colorado. The Tribune, Our Community News, and the Colorado Springs Gazette serve the newspaper needs of the area in 2004.

MONUMENT FIRES

*F*ires have destroyed many buildings in the Town. Most all were never rebuilt. On Aug. 18, 1889 on a Sunday morning, three business houses on the north side of Second and Washington Streets were destroyed. All who were at church came to help, the women carrying buckets of water to the men. The store of Will Lierd in the Dunchee block on the south side of the street, and the Dr. Bonnett drug store and office on the north side were saved. In 1894 the firehouse was called the Hook and Ladder House.

On Feb. 27, 1904 the Park Hotel and Post-office burned. Mr. Francis Bell was postmaster, also clerk of the Presbyterian Church. All church records up to this time were burned.

These buildings were on Front Street south of Second Street. I am not sure about the date, but about this same time the Iron Side Hotel burned. This was near the park.

On April 9, 1920 the Monument Post-office burned again. This was located on the south side of Second Street and west of Washington Street. It was a two-story frame building with living quarters upstairs, with a store and post-office downstairs. Mrs. Ida Betz was Postmaster. Two elderly men were burned to death in this fire; namely, Sam Putman and Bail Simpson. Rumors at that time were that one of the old men upset a coal oil lamp that started the fire.

In the winter of 1921 the Hunter building, which was the original dress-making shop of Mrs. Limbach, burned. This was on the corner of Front and Second Streets. The upstairs was used for sleeping rooms for the men that worked for the Doyle Ice Company. The Jim Travis family lived downstairs and operated a restaurant. Fortunately no lives were lost.

On March 24, 1922 the Monument Hotel burned. Roy Petrie and wife, Nellie, were operating the hotel at this time.

The Dr. McConnell drug store and office burned in the 1940's. It was being used as the Grange Hall at this time.

Monument's fire alarm in the early years was by ringing the Presbyterian Church bell, which was on a high tower east of the church. Many times when the young folks were having fun and wanted to see excitement they would ring the bell in the middle of the night then run, hide, and watch the people running around trying to find the fire. In 1931 the Town bought a chain and lock for the church bell to prevent unnecessary ringing.

The Monument Volunteer Fire Department was organized in 1949. Each year since then it has made many fine Improvements. They had remodeled the fire station in Town (once Lierd's store, now the High Country Store) and had good fire-fighting equipment. A new station was built on Woodmoor property in 1976 with many improvements since, including three change outs of major equipment. A new Tri-Lakes Fire Protection District was formed in 1977 with the station moving to Hwy. 105. A new replacement firehouse was built and a ladder-truck added in 2000. New stations are in the works with one almost completed on Roller Coaster Road. In all, ten major pieces of rolling-equipment have been added since 1977 as well as many new firefighters dedicated to the safety of the residents in our area.

Tri-Lakes Fire Department, American LaFrance
Pumper Engine – ca 1974.
Photo courtesy of Tri-Lakes Fire Department

CHURCHES

*I*n 1874 Monument had three churches. It was reported that the Episcopalians had engaged a number of lots to establish a church boarding school and parsonage. The Presbyterians had an organization in the Town, and the Methodists had erected a fine parsonage through the efforts of Rev. John L. Dyer. Father Dyer as he was called was very active in Monument, and other places in Colorado. He presided over the Monument circuit, which included charges at Blakely Mill, Weirs Mill, and Farmers Mill. Father Dyer was known as the "Snow-shoe Itinerant". In his book he describes building a fine parsonage in Monument. It was a frame house lathed and plastered, 16x24 feet and cost over $300.00. This is still part of the home of Lela Hagedorn's home on Jefferson Street. At Monument he preached in the schoolhouse, and in a small church which apparently had been built before the railroad station on the Rio Grande south of Town. George Newbrough cut the square-headed nails and helped build the parsonage.

On Nov. 16, 1874 Book K, page 66, a deed was recorded from Chas. Adams to Monument Methodist Episcopal Church.

Trustees John Lindsey, P. C. Castle, Wm. Lierd, Henry Teachout, and A. G. Teachout; $10.00 consideration, Lot 11, block 6, filed Jan. 8, 1875.

Father John L. Dyer

Known as the "Snowshoe Itinerate," this famed Methodist preacher built a small parsonage at 235 Jefferson St.

A self-ordained preacher, Father Dyer ministered to communities and mining camps throughout Colorado.

Photo courtesy of the Castle Rock Museum.

BAPTIST CHURCH

O n July 8, 1875 the Colorado Springs Weekly Gazette reported that on Sunday, July 4, 1875 the Baptists held two services at the Monument Schoolhouse for the purpose of organizing a church. The meetings were well attended and a church of sixteen members organized,--on July 31, 1875. Date of Articles of Monument Baptist Church filed Aug. 6, 1875, Book page 556. "Territory of Colorado, County of El Paso. To all persons whom this may come to know to all men by these presents that on the 31st day of July, 1875, H. H. Husted, J. H. Shumate, E. P. McElroy, J. W. Carnahan, and S. B. Wilson were duly elected trustees of the Monument Baptist Church in El Paso County, Colo. in accordance with Chapter XV of revised statutes of Colorado and said Baptist Church declare their work the maintenance spread of the Gospel of the church fellowship, and ordinance and the defense of the Bible truth.

Signed Mary Carnahan, Carrie H. Moffit, Adelade Carnahan, acknowledged before Henry Limbach, N. P. 8-4-1875". This church was on the south end of Washington Street. For several years the Baptists were inactive. In 1950 they began to organize again and began to hold services in the Homemakers Hall. Rev. V. H. Mitchell was the first pastor. In 1958 when Rev. Wayne Thompson came to Monument as pastor, W. E. Higby donated sixteen lots north of Third and west of Washington Streets to the Baptists. Under the direction of Wayne Thompson a beautiful brick church was built. It was dedicated April, 1960. A new parsonage was built north of the church.

Rev. Shaver was pastor for a few years. Rev. Robert Swift was the pastor in 1974.

PRESBYTERIAN CHURCH

*T*he Presbyterian Church was an active church in the beginning of 1874. H. B. Gage and Chas. Taylor were the first two ministers mentioned in the notes of April 11, 1879, Book 25; page 460 reads "Incorporation of Presbyterian Church of Monument, State of Colorado, and County of El Paso S. S. I, A. T. Blachly, of the Town of Monument do solemnly swear that at a meeting of the Monument Presbyterian Church held at Monument, Colo. aforesaid on the 19th day of Dec. 1878 for that purpose, the following persons were duly elected trustees of said church for the period of one year; O. P. Dunlap, A. T. Blachly, R. J. Gwillim, A. G. Teachout, and F. R. Ford. I further certify that the said church adopts its corporate name "Presbyterian Church of Monument" and at that meeting I acted as chairman. Subscribed before Henry Limbach N. P. 3-10-1879". The big bell of the church was first on a high tower east of the church. In the early years when one of the Monument pioneers passed away the bell was tolled once a minute for as many times as the person's age. The last time it tolled was in 1914 when my grandmother Christine Olfs passed away at the age of 71. The church was dedicated free of debt June 6, 1881 and Dr. Bliss of Denver preached the sermon.

Ministers through the years were Rev. Chas. B. Taylor, Sam Taylor, J. E. Lydia, D. W. Reaugh, J. B. White, J. M. Wylie, Rev. Gaines, Rev. Prichett, R. J. Hassdedt, Rev. Haines, Rev. Freeze, Leo Lake, Rev. Teed, Rev. McClure, Geo. Dageinakes, and J. Morgan McKelvey. Rev. Hassdedt built the south portion of the C. E. building while he was minister. The lumber used to build it was from the Gwillimville School. Later it was enlarged on the north side of the building. Rev. Hassdedt did most of the work when the new parsonage was built. The first parsonage was just north of the church where the Columbine Antique store was in 1974.

CATHOLIC CHURCH

*I*n 1900 the community had several Catholic families. The Priest came from Colo. Springs. They had no church but had mass in one of the family's home. Then had mass in the Woodman Hall. The hall had an old baby grand piano and that was used as an altar. Mrs. Dr. McConnell was not a Catholic but a good, Christian woman. She knew those good people needed a church so she donated the lots where the church was in 1974. Mr. Fred Schuett, who lived here and was a carpenter, built the church in 1911. The first priest was Father Chas. Hagus, and the second, Father Felix Abel. Other priests through the years were Rev. G. Raber, Rev. Andrew C. Murphy, Rev. James Gillick, Rev. James, Rev. Walter Steidle, and Rev. Chas. Rueter, Walter R. Jaiger, and Father Dresen. Families who were Charter members were Mitchell Lavelett, Jule Aubuchon, Sophia Wiscamb, Louise Ruppert, John Dolan, Patrick Murphy, Jim Pettigrew, Joe Lorraine, Ruel Aubuchon, Mary Brady, and Tom Long.

ASSEMBLY OF GOD CHURCH

*I*n 1961 a church was established with only four members, namely; Fern Webb, Lois Holder, Anna Ellis, and Fannie Ellis. Rev. Munyan was pastor. Their first services were in the Homemakers' Hall, then in a building north of General Garage. This building was not very well kept up and when it rained it leaked quite badly. The members said they "really had showers of blessings", evidently they did for their membership increased and they bought a large building that had to be moved from the Academy grounds. Lots were purchased from the Ellis sisters and the building was set on the corner of Second and Jefferson Streets. Rev. Kastel was pastor when the building was moved to Monument. With the work of several pastors and the members, today in 1974 it is a beautiful church. Pastors through the years were Rev. Munyan, Rev. Kastel, Rev. Green, Rev. Shaffer, Rev. Little, and Rev. Golaz at the present time.

St. Peters Catholic Church built in 1911, now a toy shop.

The Presbyterian Church – ca 1879.
No early photos of other churches were available at printing.

THE CALABOOSE

*T*own minutes of Sept. 7, 1800 state that the Town had a committee to make plans to build a calaboose. On Oct. 4, 1880 the committee reported the estimate for building the calaboose would be $150.00. The Town appointed a committee of three consisting of R. C. Elliott, Henry Limbach, and Chas. Tiner to build the calaboose but not to exceed in cost more than $125.00 and to be put on Lot 8, Block 8. In March 1881 they started to build and the committee authorized to spend whatever amount was necessary beyond the $125.00 previously allowed for completion. At first it was just one room about 9x12 feet. In 1887 the Town voted to partition it. In 1887 the Town Magistrate and Mayor were given permission to procure as many balls and chains, as they deemed necessary. The bills turned in for the building were: Labor, $35.00, iron for windows, $16.50, nails, $32.00, ties for foundation, $5.60, bankingup and stove, $4.00, blankets, $3.50, shingles and siding, $40.00. At first it just had a dirt floor; six years later a wood floor was put in. The calaboose was used mainly for drunks and tramps that had no money for a night's lodging. In 1895 people began to call it a jail. It was moved twice; the first time from original site to north of the school where Junior High is, then in 1920 to Washington Street. It was torn down in 1943. In 1894 and 1895 Town Marshall was paid $40.00 a month.

THE BASEBALL TEAM & BARBER SHOP

*M*y brother, George Hagedorn organized Monument's baseball team in 1914. Iven Fulker was manager. The players were: Turner, Smith, Dan Davidson, Bill Connell, Geo. Hagedorn, Wilbur Fulker, Roy Gaunt, Jack Roser, Tom Connell, Bryan Hagedorn, Bud Connell, and Marion Hagedorn.

Many of the teams they played were from Colo. Springs. In 1916 Monument won the El Paso County championship. In those days the team had to make their own expenses, and there was no charge for the games. The team gave dances, and the Hagedorn family orchestra furnished the music. This money was used to buy the team's uniforms. Dr. McConnell always bought the balls for them. Sunday was church day for the women in the morning, barber shop day for the men and boys, and baseball game in the afternoon. Farmers would drive their horses and buggies or ride horse-back to town and spend the day visiting, men getting hair-cuts, and going to the baseball game. Monument at that time had a barber only on Sunday. Andy Heckers came from Colo. Springs and had his barber chair in a room in the back of Ed. Hunter's lunchroom. He had a coal stove to heat water in a teakettle. Farmers came in early to get their names on the list and wait their turn. Andy was busy from 7:00 A.M. to 7:00 P.M. Haircuts were 25 cents for men and 15 cents for boys. Mrs. Harry Dalton was an enthusiastic baseball fan. Every Sunday she was at the game sitting on an apple box behind the backstop. Her voice was strong and loud, and she would razz the visiting team pitcher and catcher until many times they were so mad they would throw the ball away. Although Monument had an excellent team the team gave Emma Dalton a lot of credit for helping to win the games! The baseball diamond was east of the schoolhouse. After the game all would go to Ed Hunter's lunchroom and buy a big ice cream cone for a nickel. The ice cream was homemade by the Hunters in a hand turned freezer.

Each Sunday morning they would make ten gallons of ice cream from good, thick cream and whole milk bought from the Monument Creamery.

The Monument baseball team,
El Paso County Champions for 1916.

From L – R:

Roy Guant, Jack Roser, Wilber Fulker, unknown, unknown,
George Hagedorn, The three Connell Brothers Bill, Bud, and
Tom & Iven Fulker (manager)

CHEESE FACTORY & CREAMERY

R J. Gwillim, who came from Neath So. Wales operated a cheese factory and store in 1878. It was here that the first cheese in Colorado was made. Gwillim Bros. also had a cheese factory at Gwillimville, 5 miles east of Monument. It was reported that one year Mr. Gwillim shipped a carload of 16,000 pounds of cheese to Cardiff in South Wales. In the early 1900's Carlson and Frink owned and operated a creamery in Monument. It was located just east of the Santa Fe tracks and at the time was located at the east end of Second Street. My father, P. C. Hagedorn and two sons, Bryan and Marion operated the creamery from 1911 until 1917. Selling milk and cream was the only cash income the farmer had until harvest time. The creamery shipped several loads of milk a day by rail. To keep the milk fresh and sweet each can of milk was placed in a canvas jacket and the jacket filled with ice. One could always tell when it was suppertime in town by seeing the children walking to the creamery with a gallon, or half-gallon syrup pail to get milk for supper and next morning breakfast. Milk sold for 10 cents a gallon, and 5 cents for a half-gallon. It was good whole milk that one could skim an inch of cream off of in the morning. Frink Creamery made several thousand pounds of cheese a year. The cheese was known as Black Diamond cheese made from good whole milk and cream. It was shipped all over the United States. Mr. and Mrs. Andrew Cobel operated the creamery for several years.

Florence Barnhardt Cobel was known as being the best cheese maker in Colorado. Roy Tinsely and his brother operated the creamery for four years. In 1930 the creamery was torn down and milk trucked to Frink Creamery in Larkspur, Colo.

The Monument Creamery with milk being delivered by farmers. During the winter months and between harvests, the creamery was a major source of income for those with a dairy cow or two.

Roy Tinsely (L) and his brother holding a wheel of "Black Diamond" cheese which was shipped all over the USA.

Milk lid clamps made and sold by J. M. Umberger and Vern S. Perrine, both of Monument – 1925.   A paper bag advertisement.

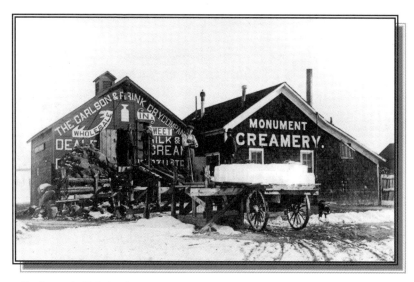

Carlson & Frink Creamery receiving an ice delivery – ca 1906.

THE MONUMENT NURSERY

*M*onument Nursery was three miles west of Monument at the foot of Monument Rock and Mt. Herman. Mr. Walter Schrader was the first superintendent of the government nursery. In 1907 Mr. Schrader spaded up a 50 foot square patch which was the first seed bed of the nursery. In 1938 the nursery required as many as 60 men to operate. The first step in growing the trees was obtaining the seed. This was done by gathering the cones. Men would raid the squirrel hoards in the woods each Fall and get two to ten bushels of cones from each. This was not cruel to the squirrels since only about half of each hoard was taken by the seed gatherers. The cones were hauled in sacks to the top floor of a three-story extractory and were cleaned of twigs and dirt. Then they were dumped on hoppers to the next floor and spread on wire racks stacked tier on tier around the room. A specially constructed hot air furnace was turned on and the room temperature held to 200 to 300 degrees for three to four days. The cones would open and much of the seed fell to the floor where it was caught in tarpaulins. The cones then were placed in a rotating cylinder and the remaining seed shaken out. The seeds were then run through a fanning mill to remove the tiny wings adhering to each seed and were finally sacked for storage. The cones would yield from one-half to two pounds of seed to the bushel.

The shelled cones were mixed with coal and used as fuel for the extractory furnace. The nursery had a 15x20-foot mouse and insect proof house that had $5,000.00 worth of seed in 1938. Most of the trees were grown for order for certain forestations. The seeds were sown so as to produce an average of 100 trees to the square foot. The seedbeds were four feet wide and each covered one-acre. The nursery had growing in 1930 several million cedars. The cedars required special treatment. The seeds were soaked in damp moss for a year before planting, and then they would remain in the ground 8 months before the germinating.

The seeds were sown with an ordinary garden planter pulled along chalk line guides. The little trees were transplanted at least once. After one or two years in transplant beds they were dug up, the roots packed in wet moss, and wrapped in bundles of 2000. When the trees were removed from a bed, the ground was re-plowed and sown with a mixture of oats and cowpeas, then this was plowed under and the ground left fallow for one year.

The Monument Nursery was established primarily to provide new trees for the reforestation of 15,000 acres of timberland in the vicinity left barren by the disastrous Mt. Herman forest fire in the 1880's. The Mt. Herman burn was completely reforested by 1926.

Two million trees were produced and shipped annually from the nursery. There were 25 million seedlings always growing in the nursery. Trees were shipped through the Rocky Mountain west to the shelterbelts stretching from the barren Dakota's to the plains of Texas. The trees grown were Douglas Fir, Western Yellow Pine, Engleman Spruce, Limber Bristle Cone, Blue Spruce, And Rocky Mountain Red Cedar. Mr. Schrader retired in 1943 after thirty-six years as superintendent of the nursery.

Ben Bovard, who has lived near and in Monument all his life and worked at the nursery, was honored in 1965 with a banquet, given a gift, and honor certificate which states "To Ben Bovard who worked 43 years aiding the culture of trees".

Joe Eiseworth operated a government sign shop making government signs, which employed several men.

Other supervisors at the nursery over the years were Earl Erickson, Bernard Abrahams, Jess Fox, Ray Johnson, Donald Oliver, and Edgar Phalpant. The Civilian Conservation Corps (C.C.C.) had a large camp at the nursery. It was established in 1933 and was a camp for young boys who, during the depression, had no work. They were paid for working at the nursery, also given schooling.

Most of the boys came from Texas and Massachusetts. The camp was abandoned when World War II was declared. The nursery closed in 1965, and moved to Basalt, Colo. where more water could be obtained for Irrigation and could operate cheaper. In 1974 the old nursery grounds is known as Monument Environment Center.

Seal of the Civilian Conservation Corps (CCC) founded during the depression years to provide jobs/schooling for young men.

Preparing the seed bed for planting/germination – ca 1938.

Transplanting young trees to another bed – ca 1938.

A fertilizer or water spreader used to nourish a freshly planted
seedbed – ca 1938.   Monument Rock is in the background.

PATRICK MURPHY
One of our most remarkable Pioneers

*P*atrick Murphy was born March 16, 1821, in Cork County, Ireland. He left Ireland in the middle of the afternoon April 21, 1864. It took fourteen days to cross the ocean in the ship named "The Kangaroo". It was among the oldest steamers at that time, Mr. Murphy in a joking way said he came to America to see the finery and pretty girls. Evidently he was hard to please for he never married. He landed in New York, went from New York to Nashville, Tennessee, then on to St. Louis, Missouri. He walked up the Mississippi River then on to Ft. Lewis.

He could not be a member of the regular army during the Civil War because he was not an American citizen, but he could be a cook in the army. He was a cook at Ft. Bent, Colo. when the war ended. While he was cook, he and Joe Pettigrew became good friends. Joe was a member of the Union Army. He was also one of our pioneers.

Mr. Murphy was a small, wiry man perhaps about 100 pounds. A great walker; when he left Ft. Bent he walked across country to the Divide. One night on this trip he was tired and weary so he took his blankets from his pack and went to sleep on a hillside. In the morning when he awoke and started again a great and sudden surprise came to him.

Just as he reached the top he saw Indians at the foot of the hill, on the other side. They were packed and painted ready for war. Mr. Murphy knew that if he turned back the Indians would find him. He boldly walked down the hill, through the camp, and kept on his way. The Indians did not do or say a thing. They simply looked astonished and muttered to one another.

When he reached the Divide he knew this was the place, as the grass was high and thick, and there were many buffalo herds. He homesteaded his place, which was about six miles east of Monument. In 1870 after he had his homestead, he walked back to Ft. Bent to tell Joe Pettigrew about the fine country and Joe came and homesteaded, his place is still known as the Pettigrew place on Highway 83. Mr. Murphy built a two-room cabin with a large fireplace at one end. Shortly after he built the cabin he walked to Fountain, Colo. and bought three cows for $360.00. Mr. Murphy's first friend here was Bob Ireland, a fine-looking man. Mr. Murphy always said, "Good looks makes a fine neighbor".

Mr. Murphy could neither read nor write, but had a sharp mind and quick wit. He worked with a couple of surveyors carrying the chain and stakes. He overheard the two surveyors talking one day that some land joining his place could be filed on. The two men planned to go to Denver in a couple of days to file a claim on it. That night Pat changed his clothes, took out walking to Denver and was coming out of the Court House with papers for the land when the other men were going up the steps. He often walked to Colo. Springs and Monument with a large basket of eggs to trade for groceries. If some neighbor came along with a team and asked him if he wanted a ride he would say, "No, thanks, I haven't time. I'm in a hurry". He could out-walk a team of horses.

When St. Francis Hospital was in a boxcar by the railroad tracks he had blood poisoning in his hand and was their first patient. When he passed away at age 105 he was the oldest member of the Knights of Columbus in the world, the oldest man in the State of Colorado, and the oldest rancher in the State of Colorado. He lived on his ranch until he was 101 years old.

When he was 100 years old he rented his farmland to Tom Long. Two men with two, six-foot binders were cutting the grain on his place and Mr. Murphy was shocking it, keeping up with the binders. He loved children and to have company; he always kept candy to give to all the children. Monument planned a big celebration for Pat on his 100-year birthday, on St. Patrick's Day, March 17, 1921. But Monument had one of the worst Spring blizzards it ever experienced so the party was postponed. At 100 years of age he was very sharp and alert, quick, and lively, walked as straight as any young man; all who knew him dearly loved him.

When he was 100 years of age he was standing on the steps of the Higby store looking towards Pike's Peak and two young men were watching him, thought they would be smart and said to him, "Old man, do you see that Jack rabbit on the top of the Peak?" Mr. Murphy with his Irish wit replied "No, by Gawd, I don't see him but I can sure hear him thumping his hind legs".

At 101 he ran a race in the main street of Monument with a man many years his junior and won, and danced at a dinner given in his honor that night. At 102 Mr. Murphy climbed half-way to the summit of Pike's Peak and was only dissuaded from completing the trip through the intercession of a younger man who was accompanying him who told Murphy he was giving out.

When he left his 1,100-acre ranch he made his home with Mr. and Mrs. James Pettigrew for a while, but later went to the St. Francis Hospital to live, where his Irish wit and jigs made him a favorite with the nurses.

He was a devout Catholic; he was a member of St. Peter's Church at Monument. He died July 3rd, 1926 at 105 years, 4 months, and 13 days of age. He is buried in the Spring Valley Cemetery near his home.

Joe Pettigrew & Pat Murphy taking milk to the creamery.

THE HIGBY FAMILY

*T*he J. W. Higby family came to Colorado and homesteaded in the area of Eastonville in 1888. They moved to Monument and opened the Higby Mercantile Co. in 1900.

William E. his son after he graduated from East Denver High School in 1906 worked for his father in the store.

W. E. Higby was known by everyone as Gene. He was very interested in public affairs and his public career began in 1910 when he was elected Treasurer of Monument. In 1912 he was elected Mayor, and served continuously for 25 years. In 1912 he was also elected Republican precinct committeeman and served continuously for 55 years. In 1920 he was elected to the Board of School District 38, a job he held for 15 years.

In 1932 he entered State government service as a State Representative from El Paso County and held that seat until being elected in 1940 to a four-year term as State Senator. His Senate career ended in mid-term as in 1942 he was elected Lieutenant Governor. In the next election year he was a candidate for the Republican gubernatorial nomination but lost a four-way contest for designation at the State Assembly. He ran for Lt. Governor again and was elected. In 1948 he was named to the Colo. Springs Board of Health, a job he held for ten years.

In his duties as Lieutenant Governor, Mr. Higby was the first person in 70 years to preside over both the Colorado House and Senate as he served as Speaker of the House, a job to which he was elected unanimously.

The Higby Livestock Company raised Hereford cattle and at one time had a spread of about 4,000 acres. W. D. Higby (Dave), his son, managed and operated the cattle company.

Dave and son, W. F. Higby (Bill) still operate the Higby Livestock ranches (1975).

W. E. Higby's other son, James E. Higby, is a pilot for Continental Airlines. Sally Higby, daughter of Dave and Edith Higby, was chosen "Girl of the West" of the Pike's Peak or Bust Rodeo Aug. 8, 9, 10, 11, in 1962. She was chosen because of her beauty, personality, talent, ambition, and outstanding horsemanship.

The Higby Mercantile Store was in continuous operation for 67 years. Four generations of the Higby's have been Mayors of Monument; J. W. Higby in 1901; W. E. Higby; W. D. Higby, and W. F. Higby, and three generations have been members of the Lewis Palmer School Board.

W. E. Higby's wife was the former Blanche David. She passed away during the 'flu epidemic in 1919, when Dave and Jim were small children. Mrs. Emily Higby, W. E.'s mother moved back to Monument and was mother and grandmother to the children. Mrs. Emily Higby was a very kind, gracious and generous lady. She never tired in giving her time, talents, and finances in helping the community. Her philosophy of life was "Cast your bread upon the waters and it will be returned". She bought the first upright piano for the Presbyterian Church. All the beautiful Pine trees that are on the school grounds she bought, and paid for the planting of them. These stately evergreens are a living memorial to her.

Higby's Mercantile – ca 1900. Gene Higby 2nd from (R).

Gene Higby holding 1st issue of Lake View Press – ca 1953.

The Higby Mercantile – ca 1957. Now the Chapala Bldg.

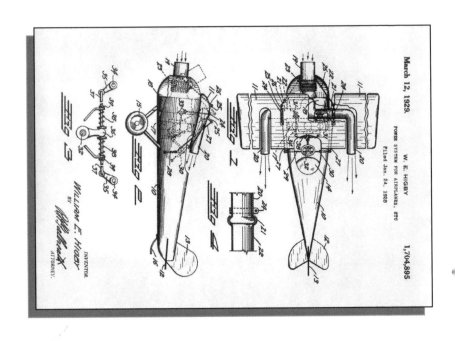

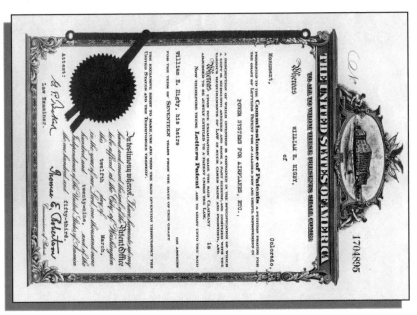

The Patent & Patent diagram for W. E. Higby's Jet Aircraft.
Patent granted on 12 March, 1929. An idea ahead of it's time.

A MONUMENT, WORLD WAR II HERO
James Newbrough

*J*im Newbrough, as we all call him, is the great-grandson of David McShane, one of the early pioneers of Monument and grandson of Mr. George Newbrough who came here in the 1860's. He is the son of the late Irvin and Elsie Newbrough.

Jim was born in Monument, Colo. Feb. 15, 1921 and has lived here all his life, with the exception of when he was in the U. S. Army and a few years on the Western Slope when he was a telegraph-line man.

The article below was "printed" in the "YANK MAGAZINE" of Dec. 13, 1943. Items in italics have been added for clarity.

"THE MUNDA AIR STRIP BATTLE"

*T*he following took place on July 28, 1943 on O'Brien hill, on the island of New Georgia which is located in the Northern Solomons of the South Pacific. The island of Guadalcanal is about 197 miles E-SE of New Georgia. The fighting had been going on for days. The morning of the 28th Newbrough's unit the 1st battalion, 161st infantry regiment was alone on the hill having been cut off.

On the right-flank center of O'Brien hill was a light machine-gun with both gunners gone; one sick and the other momentarily absent at the start of the attack. Manning the gun was the ammunition carrier, a sandy-haired, drawling, buck private named James Newbrough, of Monument, Colo.

"When the attack started Newbrough was on the gun. A Jap in front of them yelled "American Cowards". "The hell you say," Newbrough snorted. "Come on out and fight," yelled the Jap, tossing a rock.

"Come on in and get me," said Newbrough.

The Jap and his comrades thought that over threw a few more rocks and then screamed, "Here we come". Three of them sprang out with "*Nambu*" .25-caliber light-machine guns, which they fired as they rushed Newbrough's position. Two of them died in their tracks; the third ran.

Newbrough, alone on the gun, kept it going constantly. Nobody, even he knows how many belts of ammunition he expended. As the gun continued to fire, it attracted more and more attention until it seemed that Newbrough was the only target. Bullets, *some of them explosive*, splattered into everything, cutting down the *canvas* shelter-half on top of him and clearing the underbrush from around him.

Newbrough unfastened the traversing mechanism and crouching low, sighted along the under-side of the barrel so that no part of him was above the level of the gun itself. With his hand over his head he hung onto the trigger and raked the ground before him. His gun corporal, Dick Barrett of Roseburg, Wash. managed to get through to him with ammunition when the supply was almost exhausted, and PFC. Hollis S. Johnson of McKensie, Ala. came up to cover him with a Browning Automatic Rifle (BAR).

Newbrough, a shy kid, with a country brogue and the faintest show of a beard, probably saved the battalion that day. *To the men involved, the fight seemed to go on for hours. However, it ended at 10:45 AM with only forty-five minutes passing from the start of the Japanese assault.*

The attack, once stopped, was not repeated. The battalion smashed it, but not until other units approached from two sides did the Japs see proof that their case was hopeless, and withdrew in the late afternoon. With its ordeal over, the battalion took Christian Hill against little opposition and advanced 800 yards through the jungle before darkness halted it. Jim was awarded a Silver Star with Oak Leaf Cluster.

The Munda airstrip was captured on August 5, 1943.

Private James Newbrough demonstrating his fighting position on the morning of July 28, 1943. Pvt. Newbrough was awarded the Silver Star w-Oak Leaf cluster for his heroic action that day. Newbrough was also awarded two bronze battle stars for action on Guadalcanal.

M1919A4 Air-Cooled .30-caliber Machine Gun.
The traverse mechanism is located between
the two rear tripod legs.

FRED W. SIMPSON & 'OLD DISAPPEARANCE'

*I*n October, 1922 the Monument farmers felt better after the slaying of the huge mountain lion by F. W. Simpson that for years had been killing calves and young stock. With the aid of his dog, Rover, Fred Simpson tracked the lion for three hours over the snow to a point on Hay Creek, five miles west of Monument where the lion was treed and brought down by a .22 caliber bullet through his brain. "Old Disappearance" as the lion was named by the ranchers, had killed more than 30 calves just prior to Simpson tracking him down. Wilbur Doughty, a rancher living near Hay Creek section at that time, was the heaviest sufferer from "Old Disappearance's" killings. For his efforts, Simpson was awarded a bounty of $25 made good by the Denver Post newspaper.

The lion weighed 160 pounds and measured eight feet two inches tip-to-tip with paws five inches across. It was estimated the lion was more than 15 years old as a number of his teeth had been broken off and scars on his skin indicated a considerable age. The lion had been seen within a mile of Monument many times. Mr. Simpson took the lion to a taxidermist and had it mounted and for years it was on display in the A. E Fox Cash Grocery store on Front Street in Monument. "Old Disappearance" now resides on permanent display at the Lucretia Vaile Museum located in Palmer Lake.

Fred Simpson, Rover & "Old Disappearance" – 1922.

"Old Disappearance" & Fred Simpson. (R)

"HOW TIME AND PROGRESS HAVE CHANGED OUR WAY OF LIVING"

*T*his ordinance was published in a Denver newspaper January 1903: "Be it ordained by the Board of Trustees of the Town of Monument. Section 1; No railroad locomotive, railroad engine, car, or train of cars, no automobile or other conveyance or vehicle of any kind, shall be propelled, moved, run, or operated through or in the Town of Monument or any part thereof, in or along any street, or alley there at a greater speed than at the rate of ten miles per hour.

Section 2; Any and every corporation, engineer, conductor, driver, or other person having charge of, or running, driving, moving or operating any such locomotive, engine, car, train of cars, automobile, or other horseless conveyance or vehicle of any kind, who shall violate any of the provisions of the foregoing section shall be fined not less than Five dollars nor more than One hundred dollars for each offense.

W. B. Walker, Mayor

R. C. Elliott, Clerk

The following bill was sent to the Town Board by Geo. Curtis. It was written on ruled paper in his handwriting.

"Town of Monument, Colo. Dr. to Geo. Curtis" "To damage done to wagon and harness by colliding with a post setting in the middle of Third Street in the village of Monument on the night of December 31st, 1902 Ten ($10.00) dollars."

Signed Geo. H. Curtis

In the town minutes this bill was laid on the table on Mar. 2, 1903. In checking the town minutes I did not find if the Board had ever allowed this bill. As this was on New Year's Eve, I have wondered just about all the conditions of this damage.

MONUMENT HOMEMAKERS' CLUB

*T*he club history dates back to 1910. At that time it was composed of farmers and their wives and was known as Farmers' Institute. In 1917 it was still a Farmers' club but under a county agent and Extension club leader. They had all day meetings twice a month. In 1939 the great loads of grain and potatoes that were once shipped from Monument had vanished. At that time it was entirely cattle raising and dairy country, therefore the men were not interested in Agriculture clubs and it became a ladies' Homemakers' club. The homemakers' club was the only active civic organization in Monument for many years. When Nancy Williams was president, the club had one hundred members. It always sponsored the boys' and girls' 4H clubs, Boy and Girl Scouts, helping the churches, school, and Town in any way that was needed. It is the oldest club organization in Monument and has been an active for ninety-four years.

The Monument Homemakers Club – 1938.

ROADS & ROADSIDE BUSINESSES

O n November 2, 1874 the Monument Bergens Park and Fairplay wagon road was incorporated by A. Poole, Henry Guire, Henry Limbach, C. Bunker, E. Bemis, A. T. Blachly, A. F. Woodward, and O. P. Dunlap for the purpose of constructing and maintaining a wagon road from Monument to Florissant. The route of the road was surveyed in 1875 and some grading done, but the road was not completed. Proposed road was somewhat similar to that of the present road from Monument to Woodland Park.

In 1879 another company incorporated for the purpose of building a toll road over the same route, but apparently no construction work was done. Finally in 1896 A third company was incorporated for the purpose of building a road over this route to the new mining camp of West Creek. A stage line was reported operating over this route in 1896.

The first gravel or dirt road leading from the north came through the McShane ranch. In the middle of the 1880's the road turned south and west of the Twin Pine Ranch and came around the point of Monument Lake, across the railroad at Third Street, turned south on Front Street, turned east on Second Street, and turned south on Adams Street just east of the school house.

About 1912 and 1913 when the Model T became popular, the first garage was built by W. E. Higby, and J. M. Umberger was the first mechanic. This garage was located where the Snack House was in 1974. In the 1920's J. M. Umberger built a garage on the south corner of Second and Jefferson Streets. Fred Lewis and Roberts operated this garage, too. Joes had a garage on the east Side of Front Street. These garages did a flourishing business as Henry Ford's Model T had a hard time pulling up-hill from Denver to Monument. The three restaurants and hotel did a good business, too.

The first pavement which by-passed the Town was completed in 1928. This stretch, incidentally, was one of three opened that year, and the three projects finished the paving between Denver and Colo. Springs. This by-pass of Monument hurt the business houses in Town.

Herbert Olson had the first garage on the highway. This garage was later owned and operated by G. F. McReynolds. He sold his business in 1973, which was known as the Phillips 66 in 1974.

J. M. Umberger built a large, brick garage on the east Side of the pavement and operated it for several years. Mr. Alexander and Mr. Christisen operated this garage until the highway changed its route again.

Harry and Laura Stiefel owned and operated the Green Lantern Cafe on the east Side of the highway. Aunt Laura was noted for her delicious homemade pies. Harry had a. barbershop in part of the building.

The present highway past Monument went under construction in 1948 and was opened in 1950. The last project at the Monument interchange was started and finished in 1970.

The part of the highway south of Larkspur and north of Palmer Lake in the 1930's was known, as **"Ribbon of Death"** as many accidents and deaths occurred on this narrow, steep stretch of the road, Now there is the hazardous stretch north known as "Treacherous Monument Hill".

The road known as Mt. Herman Road was built in 1924 and 1925 by the Forest Service and is maintained by them.

This would be a beautiful scenic drive when in the future it is made wider. It is only recommended to slow drivers, a jeep, or 4-wheel drive at this date as washouts are not uncommon.

The Port of Entry was opened in 1957. Carroll Jones donated land for the port on the west Side, and W. E. Higby donated land on the east Side. The port clears 40,000 trucks a month. It clears trucks at the rate of one a minute on the west side, Truck traffic is regulated 24 hours a day, and the port employs several men.

In the 1940's Chester and Lois Porter owned and operated a store, restaurant, and rented cabins on the west Side of Hwy. 105 for several years.

Carroll and Adeline Jones built the first restaurant and Texaco station on Interstate 25 in 1959. The restaurant was known as the Lamplight and was at the present Arby's restaurant location.

The Monument Garage, 1st in Monument – ca 1914.

J. M. Umberger's garage built in 1929, east side of Hwy 105.

McReynolds Garage on Hwy 105.

Umberger's with the Green Lantern Restaurant (R) – 1930.

GALLERY
OF
HISTORIC PHOTOGRAPHS

The 1st aircraft to land in Monument, a "Jenny"? – ca 1920

The Schubarth steam engine, Charlie & son Bill – ca 1905.

George Betz (front) & John Boling (R) with the 1st chain drive
delivery truck in Monument – ca 1914.

Fred Millwright taking a load of grain to market in 1918.

The 'Great' Monument Snowstorm of 1913
Looking west on Second Street with Walkers on the right.

The Higby Mercantile on Second St. is on the left – 1913.

The 1913 snowstorm with Higby's Mercantile at middle.

THE PIONEERS & THE PEOPLE

Josephus Schideler & Granddaughter, Monument area – ca 1863.
Photo courtesy of the Colorado Springs Pioneers Museum

R. C. Elliott on horse. Gentleman on (L) unknown – ca 1895.

D&RG Station Agent Harry S. Maddox, Mate, & daughter
Nettie at their Monument home – ca 1910.
Photo courtesy of Ted Colley.

Dora Schuett & her bachelor brothers.

The Schuett home built by the three brothers – ca 1900.

Piute Jim & Squaw, both good
friends of H. Limbach.

Alice & John Dolan – ca 1930.
Alice was daughter of H. Guire.

Maude Dolan-Willis at the bakery – 1917 on Second St.

Henry & Mary Ann Guire, early pioneers.

Patrick Murphy – ca 1910.

Mary Schubarth drawing water at the well behind her home once located at 273 Washington St.

Violetta & Mary Whittier with three of their best friends sitting on father Frank's automobile – ca 1921.

Stroud & Nancy Roberts
Early Monument pioneers – ca 1866.

Nate Engle's Confectionery (candy) Store on Second St.
Nate is sitting in the chair – ca 1898.

A. Bail Simpson, an early Monument Pioneer.

Bob & Bill Simpson, G-G-sons of A. B., - Dec. 25, 1947.

Photo courtesy of Bill Simpson

TWO POTATO

The 1892 Potato Bake. Park Hotel (L) & D&RG Depot (R)

A table was formed in the shape of a large rectangle surrounding
the fire pits used to bake the meat and potatoes. Diners ate
standing at "the board" – 1892.

ICE HOUSE & CHUTE

The 1st Doyle & Hanks Ice House – ca 1901.

Ice cakes going up the chute – ca 1909.

BUSINESS CONCERNS & HOMES

Higby Mercantile – ca 1900.

Roth Letterhead, Mr. Roth could take care of your needs even
after you had passed away. (Undertaking)

Letterhead for Elliott's.

The Olfs home located in the south Woodmoor Dr. area
(L) to (R): Hannah Maulsby and son Raymond, Mrs. Christina
Olfs, and son Frank Olfs – ca 1890.

The Henry Limbach home on Front St. – ca 1897.

The Betz Grocery & post office - Cora Northrup & Sam Putman
Once located on Second St. and west of Washington St. Putman
and Bail Simpson died in a fire while sleeping upstairs – ca 1916.

On Second St., the home of Col. & Mrs. Ford, later the home of
Dr. & Mrs McConnell. The house was the first in town to have
modern plumbing. Note the windmill and water tank – ca 1920s.

THE SANTA FE TRAIN WRECK OF 1895

The Santa Fe train wreck of July 17, 1895, looking S-E
The trestle collapsed while under repair. There were four deaths.

Looking NW. The wreck occurred ½ mile south of Second St.
next to Beacon Light Rd. The locomotive is a 2-8-0 Baldwin.

Photos courtesy of Ralph & Norma Lavelett.

{ 131 }

MONUMENT FOLKLORE
AND COMMUNITY ACTIVITIES

*T*he young people and parents never got bored or lacked for entertainment and enjoyment in the 1800's and early 1900's; neither did it cost much money.

The young and old would have spelling matches once a month at the school house. The two captains of the teams would choose their team-mates from those present and the teams would vie to be the winners. Old timers still remember the time a grade student spelled down his teacher, P.A. Kirton, who misspelled the word "bluing". The teacher had spelled it "blueing". The ciphering matches were fun to see who could add, subtract, divide, and multiply the fastest and get the right answer. The lively debates and the literary societies were always informative and enjoyable.

There were box socials — the girls would decorate a box and pack a lovely lunch in it. The girls would keep secret what their box looked like so the boys and men bidding would not know whose box they were buying. If there was a young couple contemplating marriage the auctioneer was always able to spot the young lady's box and the boy paid a good price to get to eat with his intended bride. One night in 1920 when the Cemetery Association gave a box supper to raise money, two young men in the community, Fred Lewis and Tom Johnston, were wanting to bid on a beautiful young lady's box and the box was sold to one of the men for $50.00, which was a mighty big sum in those days.

People did not play bridge years ago; everyone played High 5. Usually every other month there was a community progressive High 5 card party at the Woodman Hall with admission of 50¢ per couple.

The Christmas season was always a happy time in Monument. The men and boys would bring in a huge evergreen tree and set it up in the northeast corner of the Presbyterian Church. The children strung popcorn and cranberries and made colored paper rings to decorate the tree. Christmas Eve the entire community took part in a program of recitations and singing, and every child got an orange and a small bag of hard candy and nuts — every child was so pleased and grateful for their candy and oranges.

Much fun was had at the community taffy pulls. The young people would meet at the W.O.W. Hall and a couple of the mothers would make a big batch of taffy. For 5¢ a large amount would be sold to each person to pull for their own taffy. It always turned out beautiful white ropes of taffy with a few exceptions when some of the boys' hands were just a little grimy, and the taffy was "tattle-tale grey". To be sure, they ate their own taffy!

In the summer the boys cut their own fishing poles from the willow trees and spent the day fishing at the Monument reservoir and the Beaver Creek. In November of each year the Monument Lake would be frozen over so that the ice would be about 3 feet thick, and before ice harvest started, the young people had skating and sled riding parties. In October the boys of the community would, with their fathers' teams of horses and wagons, haul in several big loads of wood and big pitch stumps and pile them on the southeast bank of the lake to have for their bonfires on skating party nights. The nights of the skating parties were cold but no one minded them as the floor of the wagon box was covered with a good thick layer of straw from the straw pile and then covered over with good heavy quilts mother and grandmother had made from the good parts of the old overalls. Bricks were heated in the oven all day and wrapped in gunny-sacks and put at their feet so all kept happy and warm going to the lake. They also had good heavy overall quilts for their lap robes. When they arrived at the lake the boys built the bonfire, took the heavy lap quilts and put them over the horses to keep them warm while standing. Also the quilts were cozy and warm from the animal heat when the folks started home. The bricks were piled around the bonfire so they were warm when the homeward journey began. Those who did not skate piled on the sleds and the skaters pulled them across the lake. If the moon was not bright they had coal oil lanterns that the skaters swung along with them. Many of the young people drove their teams ten miles to the skating parties picking up the neighbors who had walked to the main road to meet them.

In about 1914 when Henry Ford's model "T" with the brass radiator became popular the oldest sons of each family were given permission to drive it to the skating parties. Of course, there was no antifreeze in those days so every "Tin Lizzie", as the young people named the Ford, always had to have a big bucket so that the radiator could be drained and the buckets placed close to the bonfire so the water would not freeze and the radiator could be filled again to start home. Those first Fords did not have a starter and sometimes the boys had quite a time cranking the motor to get is started on those cold nights. All of the yester-year young folks are senior citizens now and those who still live here will tell how much fun and the good times they had without costing money. None ever minded the extra work it took to have fun. In the summer time there were hay-rack rides and picnics in the Limbach Canyon and Pine Crest, and also hiking up Mt. Herman.

HALLOWEEN STORIES

*T*he phrase "Trick or Treat" were words never heard of in the 1880's and girls never went out on Halloween night. The night before Halloween was always "clothes line night" when the boys cut all the clothes lines loose from the poles. Old timers tell that the boys never cut the lines in the middle but just from the poles so that they could be fastened up without spoiling the line. There was honor among mischief in those days — going out and tipping over all the privies was lots of fun. One Halloween night the big boys moved the big double privy from the hotel to the middle of Second Street, made large signs to put on them.

The Ladies' side said "All Democrats Vote Here" and the Men's side said "All Republicans Vote Here".

There was always a masquerade dance at the W.O.W. Hall on the 31st of October and prizes were always given for the best costume. Dixie McShane Woodworth tells the story — when she was a young lady about twelve of the young ladies planned to go to the dance all masked as ghosts. They all met at Kate Higby's home just across from the hall so all would be dressed alike and Mrs. Higby, Kate's mother, helped them get ready. While Mrs. Higby was helping the girls she also was helping Gene, her son, who had small hands and feet and could wear his mother's shoes and gloves and she was getting him dressed just like the girls. When the girls were all going out the back door Gene joined in with them. He danced and pretended to be one of the girls all evening. The girls never did notice they had an extra. When time came for the Grand March and all unmasked Gene Higby was in the middle of the group and said "Hello, girls, I've sure had a good time!" Dixie says they never did know whose face turned the reddest.

One time one of Monument's ministers had a lovely two seated surrey with the fringe on top. The large boys took that buggy on Halloween night and put it astraddle the roof of Limbach's Saloon. What a good laugh everyone had when they saw the preacher's buggy on the saloon roof; even the preacher jokingly said, "I never was that high before!" He knew most of the boys who did it. They were the Munsons, Olfs, Simpsons, and Guires so he went to them and said, "Boys, if you get up there and take it down the way you put it up and bring it home, my wife will give you the best chicken and dumpling dinner you ever ate". They did get it down, and all had another good time.

It is told that some of the young men got together one Halloween night and caught a neighbor's pet buggy horse, trimmed it's mane and tail like a donkey, and put donkey shoes on the hoofs backwards.

About the dirtiest, stinky Halloween story that was told was once when the boys had a lady teacher they did not like so they plotted a trick for her. She had a habit that as soon as school took up she went to the out-house. Halloween night the boys sawed the floor boards off even with the door so when she stepped in — down she would go. But that morning the teacher did not take her usual trip. If she had been forewarned, no one ever knew but at recess time four of the girls made a rush for the comfort station and down they went. Those four ladies still live here and how they laugh telling how they went back of the coal shed, and got some other girls to bring water to clean their shoes. The boys later told they were sorry they did not get their victim but they had a good laugh just the same. (Yours truly was one of the four girls and still remembers how sick we got and sure chucked up at cleaning our shoes. Eva Judd Campbell was one of the other girls!)

FUNNY SIDE OF LIFE

*A*lthough it was a very serious time the night in 1904 when the Park Hotel and post office burned, it had its funny side, too. The story handed down by the men that fought that fire was that Rod Walker, a business man who lived on the opposite corner from the post office, on the Second and Front side, jumped out of bed, hurriedly dressed to help fight the fire. After the men had done all they could, Mrs. Rupp had coffee and sandwiches for them. Rod, a short, small-boned man, was walking around drinking his coffee when one of the men saw that Rod had his pants on backwards and called out "Rod, be careful, you've got your pants on backwards". Rod looked at himself and said, "No problem, no problem, fellows; when I jumped out of bed and saw that big blaze everything was scared out of me for a month!"

It wasn't always the boys who were mischief makers. There were two lovely, good-looking, popular, well-respected young ladies of Monument who always loved a good laugh. They were

Nellie McShane and Maude Dolan. At one of the community dances at the W.O.W. Hall on April Fool's night the girls really had a good time. Several days before April Fool's day the girls bought several boxes of Feenamint laxative chewing gum and several boxes of Beechnut tablet chewing gum and switched the Feenamint gum into the Beechnut gum boxes. Those days every community dance had chaperones. There were two ladies who came and sat all evening on the east side of the hall, watching all the young people; they never danced or moved from their seats all night. Nellie and Maude decided they would get them to move that night, so they were the first ones to chew several tablets of Feenamint, also they were slyly passing it around to all others. About midnight things began to move. The two ladies were noticed talking seriously to each other, and soon they both got up from their seats and went for the outside door, of course there was no inside plumbing in those days. The young people said "My word, how come our watchers left us", at that time no one knew but Nellie and Maude. Very shortly nearly all the dancers instead of dancing the two-step were doing the Colorado quick-step. It was several days after April first that the trick was found out. They say no one was angry or unhappy but had good laughs for months and years.

STINKY GOOD TIMES

O ne of the popular dances was the "Chain two-step". After you had danced with your partner for a while the caller would holler "everyone join hands and circle to the right or left" and then the caller said "everyone aleman left with your right hand" and soon he called dance with your right hand partner. Nellie and Maude again had bought several packages of good strong limburger cheese, slyly joined the circle, dropped pieces of the cheese in the men's pockets, rubbed it on their hands and it rubbed off, then sneakily put their hands on boys and girls shoulders leaving some of the cheese on the clothes.

When Nellie and Maude had done all they dared they went to the kitchen and washed their hands. Soon everyone began complaining about the terrible odor. Who was it? Or, what was it? The longer they danced the warmer they got the worse the smell became. At 2:00 o'clock the dance broke up. No one got rid of the smell until they got home, washed and aired their clothes. It was said that no one ever was unhappy with the girls, but admired them for their laughs they gave to people. If by chance you would talk to some of the old timers about the limburger cheese night, they would tell you how very funny it was to see everyone turning up their noses and saying "for land's sake, what died in here?"

Another laughable, stinky, smelly story was when two 8th grade boys in 1925, namely Gritt Abbott and Abbott Waldron, Jr. caught a skunk on the Waldron ranch and took the skunk oil and put it in two Karo half-gallon syrup pails. How they stood the smell getting that skunk oil in the pails we will never know. The boys took the pails of skunk oil to school with them. No one thought anything was amiss by seeing the boys with the two pails as most all the children took their lunches to school in these kind of buckets because they had good tight lids. Once while on the bus, one of the boys opened his bucket a little and let the fumes out. In a little bit the bus driver said, "P.U., I must have hit a skunk". After school had taken up, the two boys slipped the buckets in two of the cubby-holes under the stairs, removed the lids, and quietly went back to their rooms. It wasn't long until the skunk oil fumes had penetrated the entire building. The janitor and teachers began looking for a skunk. They could not find it and everyone was getting sick from the odor so they had to dismiss school. The janitor finally discovered the buckets of skunk oil. The boys were not punished, but were asked "how did you stand to get that oil out of the skunk"? Their reply was "it was tough but we knew we would have a holiday so it was fun".

THE CIRCUS TRAIN

*T*he day the circus train came through Monument was always a big exciting time for the young people. The agent always knew the time the train would be coming so he let all the kids know about it. The train always pulled in on the siding and was there for an hour or longer, while the advertising circus crew got off and the livery wagons took them around town to paste their big billboard signs on the barns and buildings. The advertising crew always gave several free tickets to all the kids, and to all the places where they put up their signs. While the train was stopped, the clowns, Fat Lady, monkey, and elephant trainers with their animals would walk up and down the length of the train and entertain those who came to see the circus train. It was good advertising. The kids with all their free tickets were sure the parents would take them to Colorado Springs the next day. The families could not afford to ride the trains to town, so on circus days the families had their picnic baskets packed with enough food for dinner and supper, got up at 4:00 A.M., got in the lumber wagon and started for Colorado Springs. Father would put the horses in Peck's corral for the day, take their lunch to the park, and eat them out at the circus grounds. They would get started for home about 5:00 P.M., eat the rest of the lunch for their supper on the way home, and soon the kids were sound asleep on the bottom of the wagon. Next day everyone was still excited, laughing and telling all about the animals, clowns, beautiful ladies, and the men on the flying trapeze.

In the Spring and Summer the hills and fields were bright with wild flowers and Columbines in the ravines and canyons. Ben Simpson, one of the Monument home boys, tells that the first money he ever made was by selling bouquets of Columbines and wild flowers to the tourists and passengers on the trains when the trains stopped at Palmer Lake to let the people off to eat at Judd's eating house, and while the steam engine was being filled with water from the water tank. Ben was about 12 years old, and in the early morning he would be out picking Columbines and other flowers, making them into bouquets, take them to the depot, and sell them for a nickel a bouquet. Some days he would make a dollar or a dollar and a half, which was a lot of money in those days, especially for a 12 year-old whose mother had passed away when he was very small, and he did this on his own to have money for food and clothes.

Mr. Clifton Lierd said many of the boys made from 10¢ to 25¢ carrying buckets of ice from the ice houses to the saloon to cool the beer. He said he was never allowed to do this since his parents did not approve of him going into the saloon.

In 1881 the Monument saloon was fined for keeping window shades down on Sunday. At this time, too, Monument had a town ordinance that ladies should always be properly dressed when walking on the streets. According to the stories told by the pioneers, it wasn't always the kids or young people who did the devilish tricks. Monument did not have a "peeping Tom" but there was a woman who lived in town who was very much opposed to the saloons, and she was named "peeping Sal". She wanted to know who the men were who spent their evenings at the saloon, so she could give their wives a bad time. Most every night after dark she would go and peek in the windows of the saloon, and several times the men had seen her. There was a narrow one-way passage between Limbach's saloon and Rod Walker's store, and when anyone opened the door she ran between the buildings. One night Bail Simpson said, "I'll cure her of the peeping habit!" When he opened the door she ran between the buildings to the far end, and it was pitch dark. He pretended that he did not know she was there, and he walked down and relieved the pressure from his bladder all over her. That was the cure from the peeping and the end of her sarcastic remarks to the ladies whose husbands went to the saloon.

YESTERYEARS' LIVING HABITS IN
THE TOWN OF MONUMENT

W henever father paid the monthly grocery bill, the grocer always gave him a sack of candy for the kids.

Everyone kept in touch with the neighbors with the country party-telephones. The telephone lines were built by nailing 2 x 4's about 2 feet high on top of the fence posts. The telephones had cranks on them which you turned to ring your neighbor. When the phone rang all the receivers clicked for the latest news.

The grocer had large stalks of bananas hanging from the ceiling of the store. He would cut them off with a curved knife, and sold them by the dozen. There was lots of excitement one time when George Betz got in a large stalk of bananas and as he took it out of the crate curled around the stalk was a large poisonous snake! No doubt it had been there when the stalk was cut from the banana tree.

By the coal-oil barrel sat a basket of small cull potatoes to be used to stop up the spout of the coal-oil can to keep it from sloshing out. The butcher always gave away the livers, kidneys, brains, and bones from the beef, and also the cracklings after the lard was rendered.

Most every home had a wooden hammock made from barrel staves.

Peanuts were in large barrels in the grocery store, and the grocer always gave the children a handful of peanuts when the parents bought groceries. Very seldom did a home have a loaf of store-bought bread, even when bread sold at six 5¢ loaves for a quarter. Stores never sold fertilizer in fancy paper bags — it always came from the barn yard. Vinegar was shipped in by the barrel and housewives took their half-gallon fruit jars to the store to be filled.

All in the family hurried to get the evening chores done so all could listen to Amos and Andy on the battery radio, and music on the Cylinder phonograph. Every store had a large coffee grinder. The coffee beans were shipped to the merchant and he would grind and weigh what the customer wanted. One day when Clifton Lierd was a lad working for his father in the store, a customer came in to buy a couple of pounds of Arbuckles coffee. With every pound of coffee the merchant was to give a ¼ lb. of wrapped candy. Clifton made a mistake and ground paper, candy with the coffee. That night the customer brought the coffee back and Clifton made sure he just ground coffee.

The salesmen of yesteryear were called "Drummers". They always came to Monument on the train and had many trunks filled with wares for the merchant to examine. The "drummer" stayed at the hotel for 3 or 4 days as it took him that long to work the town. At night, the men of the town would congregate in the hotel lobby to visit with him and get news of the many places the drummer had been before coming to Monument.

The first packaged tobacco was "Bull Durham", which came in little cotton sacks with a draw string on the top. Chewing tobacco came in ropes, twisted and hung from a peg, and sold by the twist. The men who smoked cigarettes rolled their own, and with every small bag of Bull Durham, cans of Prince Albert, Union Leader, and Lucky Strike came small packs of cigarette papers. Most men were perfectionists rolling nice round plump cigarettes. Women didn't have time to smoke in those days, only a few did with their little clay pipes.

In the summer time all stores were well stocked with fly-catching paper. They were double sheets about 12x6 that when pulled apart were covered with sticky glue that caught the flies when they lit on it. Then there were the poison sheets of fly paper that were put in old saucers and water poured over them that the flies drank and were killed.

Flour came in 100 pound white muslin sacks that mother always made all the children's underwear and petticoats out of, and also many household articles; curtains, table cloths, and pillow cases. "Pride of the Rockies" was the favorite brand of flour. The sacks were carefully unraveled and the string was wound into large balls to be used for many things. Mothers had to boil the flour sacks in lye water to get the printed brand out of the sack, because the kids did not want their underwear to have "Pride of the Rockies" on them.

The voting booths were made of heavy tin that folded so they could be stored until the next election. The booths had a shelf with a place for the ink bottle and pen, and a place to hold the candle for light. One corner of the ballots was a black square that the number of the voter who was on the record book was put on the white side of the square, and the black corner glued over it. It was supposed to be secret vote but shady politicians sometimes found ways to get ballots and open up the black corner and compare the number with numbers in the book to see who voted for whom. No doubt, there were voting scandals back then only on a smaller scale.

Marian M. McDonough
Age 4 - 5

Mrs. McDonough was active as a writer of historical articles and books. She was a principal founder of the Palmer Lake Historical Society in 1956. She was the President of the Historical Society for 19 years as well as Director of our local museum. I dedicate this reprint effort to her and all those that volunteer their time for the benefit of all.

Editor

ca - 1902

THIS AND THAT

*T*he Hagedorn orchestra of Monument consisted of my mother and her four sons. Mother Mary played the piano; George the Cornet; Bryan the Violin; and Marion the Drums.

They furnished the music for all the dances in Monument and surrounding communities. They played from 8:00 P.M. to 3:00 A.M. for $5.00 apiece. After mother and brother, George, passed away my sister, Mildred was accompanist for brother, Bryan.

C. N. LAVELETT TRUCK LINE

*I*n 1929 Clarence Lavelett began a truck route which gathered up milk each morning from surrounding farms which were approximately 12 miles east and north of Monument, and trucked it to the Frink Creamery at Monument. When the creamery closed the milk was trucked to Larkspur, Colo. Also a double-deck truckload of milk was picked up each morning and taken to the Colo. Springs creameries. In the 1940's when sons, Ralph and Leonard became old enough to drive the trucks Clarence enlarged the truck business and operated under PUC #418 and PUC C-430, and was known as the Lavelett Trucking Fuel and Feed, which sold stock-feed and hauled and sold lignite coal from the Pike View mine. The mine was located about 12 miles south of Monument. Hard coal was trucked in from Canon City. From the last of September to the first of November trucks were making 3 trips a day from ranches hauling cattle, pigs, and sheep to the Denver market.

This was within a 15-mile air radius of Monument. C. N. Lavelett said out to D. D. Young. Other truckers in this vicinity were Vern Perrine, T. F. Garrett, and Earl Engel.

FOX CASH GROCERY

A.E. Fox owned and operated a grocery store in the original Elliott store for many years. In the 1921 school annual his ad reads;

"Fox's cash grocery, staple, and fancy groceries. Your brand of cigars, Fine candies, Paramount phonographs, and Records".
A. E. Fox sold to Robert Kuhlman, who operated a fine grocery store in this same building and rented freezer lockers for many years.

Some of the ads in the school's second annual "The West Wind" in 1922:

In 1922 the Equity Produce and Mercantile was doing a good business. It was a farmers' Co-op store located on Washington Street. J. R. Close and C. C. Garrett operated it. Elsie Romack Newbrough was a clerk in 1918.

The White Front Shoe and Harness Repair Shop on Front Street with E. Vaiden Hunt as proprietor. Ad states he had the only complete modern shop between Denver and Colo. Springs. He would receive and deliver shoes by mail.

"Crowe Ranch Herefords" owned by Mosely and Dunn at Husted, Colo. just 6 miles south of Monument. "Registered Bulls for Sale".

E. Vaiden Hunt

Proprietor
White Front
Shoe & Harness
Repair – ca 1922.

HISTORY ADDENDUM, DAVID McSHANE

*D*avid McShane and wife Catherine started west intending to set up a farm in Kansas. On the way, many travelers were bound for "Pikes Peak or Bust." The gold rush fever took hold in 1860 and he joined in. McShane first camped in the Monument area in 1861 while on his way to prospect for gold in Summit County. In his quest for the shining metal, he visited gold camps in New Mexico, Colorado, and Montana. On an expedition to the San Juan Mountains in the winter of 1861 they became snowed in and resorted to eating their pack oxen. At another camp in N.M., McShane told of the profiteering that sometimes took place. A man brought in 200 sacks of flour, another a stock of liquor and ale. Both expected to make a killing when the mines opened in the spring. The man with the flour would take only silver or gold. Hungry miners resorted to taking the flour by force. A deal was worked out whereby those with gold or goods would buy or use the goods as collateral to provide flour to those with no funds. McShane got only two sacks of flour for a wagon easily worth $100. The saloon keeper did not fare as well as thieves drank much of his stock. The man charged was later acquitted at trial. The jury drank a goodly portion of the keepers remaining ale in trying the case. McShane's gold fever ebbed in 1864 and he left for Iowa reuniting with his patient wife and as yet unseen son.

In the spring of 1865, he returned with his wife and child and settled on a 160-acre homestead just west of the present D&RG tracks. He built a log cabin on, as noted in his memoirs, "the best grazing country on earth." He relates in his memoirs that "all five of his daughters married Republicans and the father, being an ardent Democrat made the remark, "The Devil owed me a debt and paid it off in giving me five Republican sons-in-law."" McShane would become a prominent builder throughout the county. He wrote that his mining exploits were not "extensive" (profitable), but his presence significantly enriched Monument, El Paso County, and our area history. McShane died on May 17, 1907.

Excerpted from an article by: Mr. Bill Hemingway, Empire Magazine 9/21/1975

NEWER DEVELOPMENTS

*I*t was June 24, 1954 when word was received that the Air Force Academy would be built approximately 6 miles south of Monument. Since then the Town and surrounding acreage has several new developments. Woodmoor community started in 1963 under the leadership of Steven N. Arnold. What once was farmland and sold for $11.00 to $15.00 per acre sells for several thousands of dollars per lot. There are many beautiful homes among the pines, also an 18-hole golf course, four-story Country Club, swimming pool, tennis court, a 50 acre lake, and a Western Motel Inn. The Mine Shopping Center is at the foot of Lake Woodmoor dam. It is east and north of the Monument interchange of 1-25. The shopping center had its grand opening March 28, 1971. The following businesses opened that day: Woodmoor Hardware, L & L Super market, Woodmoor Village Drug, Cork & Bottle Liquors, Heritage Square Gift Shop, Electronics Service, BusyBee Cleaners, Frank's Town & Country Hair Design, Woodmoor Barber, Bank of Woodmoor, Woodmoor Realty, and Woodmoor Chevron Station. Most all of the businesses above have closed, been replaced, moved or changed their name excepting the Bank of Woodmoor.

Norman Bodinger and John Hughes opened a private residential development May 1958 south of Town and west of the Rio Grande tracks and is known as the Pine Hills development.

Just west of Monument Wilbur Carrothers sold land and several new homes have been built in that area.

Stuckey's Pecan Shoppe south of Monument located near the Old Pring Station area opened in October 1965. Stuckey's was replaced by a Diamond Shamrock truck-stop and gas station.

The National Carvers' Museum, which was approximately 4 miles south of Monument, had its grand opening July 1974. Unfortunately the museum closed its doors in the mid 1990s.

Plateau Natural Gas Company was given a franchise in 1960. The first time Monument had natural gas was Feb. 5, 1962. Propane fuel was used prior to this time and stored in tanks.

Monument voted bonds for a sewer system, Aug. 6, 1962.

The cost was about $78,000.00. A lagoon was constructed south of Town near the Monument Creek.

A Conoco Station was built near the highway in 1964.

The decade of the 1990s brought major change to the highway business district. McDonalds came to town followed soon by Burger King, Taco Bell, and Arby's restaurants. All are on Hwy 105. The L&L supermarket closed with the coming of Safeway and King Soopers. Many new businesses opened in the Safeway center and are doing well. The Monument Plaza center on the west side of highway 105 is full of all manner of shops and businesses. Real estate prices boomed and the population swelled throughout the area. The historic downtown shopping areas have been renovated with many fine establishments located there. The retail needs of the community are well met now and better than ever before. No less than six banks now serve our community. The population is such that a new high school to accommodate the growth is under consideration. There are many fine service organizations serving the community in a wide area of concerns from the arts, history, the needy, and beyond. A Home Depot store will open soon. Many new churches have come to the area to fill spiritual needs.

NUDISTS

*T*he Nudists had a retreat one-mile south of Monument, on Mrs. Judd's old farm in 1954. The cold wind from the top of Pike's Peak and the sun hiding behind Mt. Herman early in the afternoons kept it too cold for them, so they were only there for about a year. It was named "Roaming Acres".

RED ROCK RANCH

*I*n 1953 Col. Hugh Nevins and his wife, Mary, bought a 210-acre spread known as the Red Rock Ranch. Since then they have added on to the north and south and now it contains 1500 acres. The ranch is approximately 3 miles north and west of Monument, nestled at the foot of the mountains. In 1975 it has 41 beautiful homes, and has its own water system.

The main road, off of Hwy. 105, is paved. There are beautiful red rock formations on the ranch namely; the one the pioneers called the "Old Washer Woman" and "The Pink Lady".

The ranch is a higher end housing development with most houses on several acres or more.

COLORADO ESTATES

*T*he Colorado Estates, which is 3 miles north of Monument and east of the Elephant Rock, is the site of many new homes.

The Colo. Estates developers are Jack Wogan, Ken Barber, and Bob Moore.

MONUMENT'S FIRST VETERINARIAN HOSPITAL

*R*ichard H. Beck, D. V. M. announced the opening of a practice in veterinary medicine, caring for large and small animals in October 1971. Dr. Beck, a C. S. U. graduate, first provided house call service to the area from his mobile clinic unit, and had surgery facilities available in the basement of his home. In 1972 Dr. Beck and his wife, Sally, built a new Veterinary Hospital on the corner of Third Street and Beacon

Light Road. It is an immaculate hospital, and has all the latest equipment to care for all large and small animals.

VILLAGE INN PANCAKE HOUSE

*W*hat was the original homestead of Herman Schwanbeck and later the homes of John Ryan, Matt Olson, and W. E. Higby on Highway 105 is today the site of the Village Inn Pancake House. It had it's grand opening on Feb. 12, 1973, with Mr. and Mrs. Boudreau as proprietors.

In 1975 there are several new business places on Second Street. There is a Snack Shop, Wash House, Bee 11 Sewing & Craft Shop, Record Shop, Ready to Wear, and Gingham Closet.

Virginia McDaniel opened the Ladies' Mart on No.4 Beacon Light Road in December 1974. The name of the shop was changed to MJ Design in 1975. This shop has carpeting, drapes, and all things necessary for home decoration.

On the northwest corner of the Monument Lake that the pioneers always called the Point, town homes have been built. These homes are known as "The Point". The street has been named Raspberry Lane. The first building of these homes was in April, 1973 by the Raspberry Mtn. Corporation on the west side of the Point. In April 1975 there were 42 completed homes.

ARROWWOOD SUBDIVISION

*E*ast of Monument and bordering Highway 105 there is the new housing development known as Arrowwood. Many new homes have been built among the pine trees. In the early years this area was known as the "Pinery".

THE ACADEMY ACRES MOBILE PARK

*T*he Academy Acres Campground and Mobile Park is located one-half mile north of Monument, on Beacon Light Road. Mr. Charles Nicholson built it in 1968. Others who have owned it are Howard Cloud and Betty Faux. Mr. and Mrs. Gary Collins purchased it in January 1974 and improved it so that it is known as one of the nicest Mobil Parks in the area. The grounds have 61 spaces for mobile homes, 60 spaces for campers and 40 tent sites with all modern facilities. The streets are all paved. The park has a beautiful view of the mountains to the west. During the tourist season it accommodates 50 campers per night. It has 40 mobile homes year round.

REFLECTIONS OF THE AUTHOR

*S*pace prevents recording many interesting and complete happenings or stories of the people who helped make Monument a prosperous town in the early years. The original pioneers are gone; many of their names are on markers in Monument Cemetery. Several descendants of our pioneers are still a part of our Town. Time and progress have made many changes, brought many new people and new ideas from near and far places.

The yester-years and today have combined to make Monument a memorable, historic Town.

Timeline for Monument Colorado

1820	The Long Expedition Explored the Palmer Divide Area. Discovered the Lavender Columbine, CO State Flower, in the area.
1835	The Dodge Expedition comes through, named the stream *Fontaine Que Bouillait,* later to be Mon. Creek.
1843	The Fremont Expedition names "Monument Creek."
1865-68	McShane Fort used as refuge by pioneers against Arapahoe and Cheyenne raids. Indian raids for horses and food. Some settlers killed.
1869	First post office. David McShane postmaster.
1870	Monument Hotel built-owned by Col. and Mrs. Ford. Potatoes are the chief crop. Potato Bake day (big event) held after Oct. harvest. 1st log school built.
1872	Area named Henry Station after "Dutch Henry." postmaster & proprietor of Grocery store. First Rio Grande Train through the area on Jan. 1.
1874	Jan 5, plat statement filed & town name changed to Monument. Three churches established; Episcopalian, Presbyterian, Methodist.
1875	First drug store owned by Trew Blachly. First Doctor – Frank Blachly. Western Telegraph service comes to town.
1878	Private school opened. First newspaper – The Mentor. (owned by A. T. Blachly)
1879	July 3 First Town Meeting Held in Gwillim Hall on corner of Third & Front St. 1st Mayor Henry Limbach. 1st Town Marshall W. E. Holbrook
1880	Jail (calaboose) built. Monument Journal newspaper started.
1881	Town Council called special election to bring water to town. Bonds issued Jan 2, 1882.

1882	Will Lierd built dry goods, shoes, groceries, casket & coffin store on Washington St.
1883	First Park (Limbach) deeded by Charles Adams.
1886	Cemetery deeded by C.R. Bissell.
1888	Water pipes laid by A. F. Woodward along streets and alleys & he sold the water to residents.
1891	Colorado Assembly appropriated funds for construction of dam. (Created Monument Lake)
1892	Oil street lights purchased.
1895	A blight, the "psyllid yellows," devastates potato crops.
1896	Telephone service comes to town.
1901	W. E. Doyle & Thomas Hanks leased lake for ice harvesting.
1907	Monument Nursery established for reforestation.
1910	Monument Homemakers established.
1911	1st St. Peters Catholic Church built.
1914	D. Davidson owned 1st chain driven auto.
1920	Inez J. Lewis consolidated school opened.
1922	"Old Disappearance" mountain lion shot by Fred W. Simpson. Monument Hotel burned down.
1931	Electricity arrived.
1932	Ice Harvest Company changed hands. due to crop failure.
1943	Ice Company went out of business due to weather changes.
1949	Monument Fire Dept. organized.
1950	Feb. 18 - Fort McShane Fort marker dedicated at the McShane home.
1957	Built New High School - Lewis Palmer.
1961	Natural gas now available. Assembly of God church established.
1975	Monument gets branch of El Paso County Library.
1980	New Monument Town Hall built. Lewis Palmer High School built. Old high school became Middle School. Big Red became Administration Building.

1990	Population influx begins.
1993	Safeway Center came to Monument.
1994	Lewis Palmer Middle School built.
1995	Old Middle school became Grace Best Elementary.
2000	New Post Office built on Third St.
2001	Monument Lake drained for dam repairs. Creekside Middle School started.
2002	Dam repairs completed. Lake cannot be filled due to drought.
2004	Water to fill lake still not available. Town celebrates 125th anniversary since incorporation.

Courtesy of the Town of Monument.

Index of People

Page numbers in **bold** indicate photographs.

{ *157* }

About The Author

My grandparents, John and Christina Olfs, came from Germany in 1860 and homesteaded 1-½ miles north of Monument.

My mother, Mary Olfs, and father, Philip C. Hagedorn were married in the Presbyterian Church in Monument, December 31, 1891.

I have lived in Monument all my life and am a graduate of Louis Palmer School. I married Clarence N. Lavelett, who was also a native of this area. We had two sons, Ralph and Leonard. We operated the Lavelett Truck Line for 20 years. I was Postmaster for 5-½ years.

My husband and I were 4-H leaders for 5 years and sponsored the Boy Scouts for 4 years.

The C. N. Lavelett house was known as a good time home and free boarding house, as the home was open to all the basketball team on practice nights, before and after the games, and for all other teenage activities.

Clarence, my husband, passed away in 1957.

I am not a writer and have never had any training in that line but have listened to many interesting stories of my pioneer relatives and friends. I have a large collection of pictures of my own, and received many from friends, some over 100 years old. I have always been interested in local history.

Just as an interesting hobby, and to keep myself busy, after my retirement from the accounting office in the B.X. at the Academy, I began to do research on the town of Monument. As I read, and made notes, I would tell people of the historical events of the town. Friends encouraged me to put it in a booklet. Working on it for four years has given me many hours of pleasure.

I sincerely hope all that read it will enjoy it now and in the future years.

Lucille passed from us on January 5, 1998.

She is missed.

Lucille Lavelett

Artist unknown

THE PALMER LAKE HISTORICAL SOCIETY

History Should Be More Than A Memory.

RMD